Rail freight since 1968
WAGONLOAD

Rail freight since 1968

WAGONLOAD

Paul Shannon

·RAILWAY HERITAGE·
from
The NOSTALGIA Collection

© Paul Shannon 2006

All rights reserved. No part of this publication may be reproduced, stored in a retrieval system or transmitted, in any form or by any means, electronic, mechanical, photocopying, recording or otherwise, without prior permission in writing from Silver Link Publishing Ltd.

First published in 2006
Reprinted 2008

British Library Cataloguing in Publication Data

A catalogue record for this book is available from the British Library.

ISBN 978 1 85794 264 4

Silver Link Publishing Ltd
The Trundle
Ringstead Road
Great Addington
Kettering
Northants NN14 4BW

Tel/Fax: 01536 330588
email: sales@nostalgiacollection.com
Website: www.nostalgiacollection.com

Printed and bound in Great Britain

All photographs are by the author unless otherwise credited.

Half title No 47294 passes Helsby with the T61 trip working from Dee Marsh Junction to Warrington on 6 July 1983. The first wagon is a discharged sodium tank from the Deeside Titanium plant.

Frontispiece No 90144 passes Abington with 6M73, the 1745 Mossend to Crewe RfD European service, on 14 April 1992. The load included bottled whisky from Kilmarnock for export to France via the Dover-Dunkerque train ferry.

Below The Highland Railway goods shed, signal box, signal and loading gauge at Invergordon provide a period setting for No 47519 as it arrives with the morning trip working from Inverness on 13 August 1981. The train comprises an FBB flat wagon with an empty whisky tank for the distillery and two empty MCV mineral wagons on their way to the scrap metal terminal at Evanton.

A Silver Link book
from
The NOSTALGIA *Collection*

Contents

Preface	6
1. The wagonload legacy	7
Tees Yard	31
The decline of a station goods yard:	
Cambridge Coalfields, 1978-81	38
2. The rise and fall of Speedlink	46
Train ferries	80
A Speedlink case study: Ciba-Geigy, Duxford	83
3. After Speedlink	89
European traffic	89
Domestic traffic: 'contract trains' and	
Tiger Freightways	96
Enterprise	104
Index	127

Preface

In 1968 rail freight operations in Britain were still adapting to the consequences of the infamous Beeching report. Although steam had given way to diesel and electric traction, many steam-age features and practices were slow to change. The ageing rolling-stock fleet comprised large numbers of short-wheelbase, low-capacity wagons, either with obsolete vacuum brakes or with no automatic brake at all. The rail freight infrastructure was similarly in need of modernisation: BR still served a large number of small goods yards and private sidings, often requiring labour-intensive shunting and local trip working to connect with the increasingly uneconomic wagonload network.

It was wagonload freight traffic that suffered most as the road network improved and as costs of road transport came down. A journey time of several days by rail could not compete with door-to-door transport by lorry. As more and more customers stopped using rail, BR was forced to withdraw little-used services and attribute the fixed costs of the remaining network to an ever shrinking number of flows. The wagonload system had entered a terminal spiral of decline.

The air-braked Speedlink network was a brave attempt by BR to stay in the market for less-than-trainload freight, essentially by offering a more competitive product on selected routes while abandoning those flows that could never be transported economically. However, Speedlink ultimately faced the same problems that had killed the traditional network: it was impossible to guarantee adequate loadings on local feeder services and even on some trunk trains. The 'sectorisation' of BR brought the issue into sharp focus as the revenue from wagonload customers was found to fall a long way short of the costs incurred.

Speedlink was duly abandoned in July 1991, leaving just a much reduced network for European traffic in anticipation of the Channel Tunnel.

As British Rail entered the private sector, wagonload freight was relaunched by Transrail and further developed by the new national operator, English Welsh & Scottish Railway (EWS). This was no return to Speedlink, but it represented a more flexible response to customers' needs and as such was very welcome. Under Ed Burkhardt's leadership Enterprise attracted a wide range of traffics and saw the return of regular freight trains to locations such as Georgemas Junction, Oban and Lowestoft. The early years of the 21st century saw EWS adopt a more cautious approach, with some services facing the axe, but the core network remained in place and volumes on some routes remained healthy.

This book traces the development of less-than-trainload freight over the last four decades, looking in detail at the fascinating variety of traffic flows often referred to as 'general merchandise', some of which disappeared almost unnoticed. The information has come from a wide range of sources, including personal observation as well as working timetables and other official documents when available. All dates and other details are believed to be correct, but the author and publisher would be pleased to receive any further information from readers with local knowledge.

The author thanks the photographers who supplied the archive material used in this book and acknowledges the generous help of very many railway employees, rail freight customers and fellow enthusiasts who have supplied information, arranged site visits and provided companionship over the last 30 years. Without their assistance, this book would not have been possible.

1.
The wagonload legacy

Although 1968 was a watershed year for BR as it finally rid itself of standard-gauge steam, the modernisation of the country's freight operations was far from complete. The Beeching Report of 1963 had highlighted the inefficiencies of the traditional wagonload network, where individual wagons were moved from point of origin to destination by a sequence of trains, connecting with each other at strategically placed marshalling yards. Often a wagon would take several days to reach its destination, sometimes spending more time waiting in yards than on the move. Yards contributed nothing to the railway's revenue – rather they were a drain on precious resources. Nevertheless, in 1968 some 69% of BR's freight traffic was still being moved by the wagonload network.

BR's marshalling yards were largely a product of the ambitious 1955 Modernisation Plan, which aimed to make operations more efficient by replacing more than 100 flat yards with about 50 new or rebuilt hump yards, making use of technology such as automatic point operation and rail-brakes. Unfortunately, however, most of the new yards never handled the volumes of traffic for which they were designed.

A case in point was Carlisle Kingmoor, completed in 1963 to replace a plethora of small, inefficient yards in and around the border city. The capacity of Carlisle Kingmoor was 5,000 wagons a day, but the actual throughput peaked at around 4,000 wagons before declining to unacceptably low levels by the end of the decade. In 1973 the down yard was declared redundant and all traffic was concentrated on the former up yard. Even then there was plenty of spare capacity; in 1981 the up-side hump closed and all remaining shunting was carried out on the flat.

The factors that led to the decline of Carlisle Kingmoor were representative of those facing BR as a whole. The completion of the M6 motorway to the Scottish border had made road transport more viable for Anglo-Scottish traffic, while the closure of the Waverley Route from Carlisle to Edinburgh in 1970 forced the diversion of some wagonload traffic via the East Coast instead of the West Coast main line. Industrial changes in the late 1970s brought a sharp reduction in wagonload traffic to and from Workington steelworks. In 1983 Kingmoor suffered further loss when BR withdrew all through freight from the Settle & Carlisle line.

If Carlisle Kingmoor was destined to become something of a white elephant, other projected yards from the 1955 Modernisation Plan never progressed beyond the drawing-board. For example, plans for an orbital freight route round the north side of London would have seen a major new yard at Swanbourne. In the event BR got as far as building an expensive flyover across the West Coast Main Line at Bletchley, but then abandoned its plans for an orbital freight route before any physical work at Swanbourne had started.

Wagonload-trainload split, by tonnage		
Year	Wagonload %	Trainload %
1968	69	31
1972	33	67
1977	20	80
1990	2	98

Above The Dunkerque to Dover train ferry carried large amounts of perishables traffic from southern Europe to Britain, some of which was loaded in Interfrigo refrigerated vans. Class 71 electric No E5002 arrives at Hither Green with a service from Dover in May 1968. The 9D headcode shows that the train was routed via Chatham. *J. H. Cooper-Smith*

Below Class 37 No D6833 passes Wetheral station with 7M54, the 0915 from Tyne Yard to Carlisle, on 28 June 1968. At that time the BR timetable included no fewer than seven trains a day for general wagonload traffic from Tyne to Carlisle. *Michael Mensing*

THE WAGONLOAD LEGACY

'Hymek' Class 35 No D7028 heads south on the West London line near West Brompton with an inter-regional freight bound for the Southern Region in June 1969. The seventh and eighth wagons in the train are 'Conflat' vehicles with 'door to door' containers, a system that was soon to be abandoned as the Freightliner network expanded. *J. H. Cooper-Smith*

The British Thomson-Houston Type 1, later known as Class 15, was one of the less successful Modernisation Plan designs. They were used on light freight and empty coaching stock duties in East London and East Anglia, but all were withdrawn by the early 1970s. No D8242 approaches Ipswich with an up freight on 17 August 1969, likely to have originated at Claydon cement works as it comprises Presflo cement wagons and empty coal wagons. *J. H. Cooper-Smith*

RAIL FREIGHT: WAGONLOAD

Settle & Carlisle line freight, July 1982

Up

Code	Time at Appleby	Days	Train details
6V90	0701	MSX	0557 Carlisle to Severn Tunnel Junction
8G80	0741	SX	0630 Carlisle to Bescot
6M35	0922	TThO	1647 Stevenston to Burn Naze (COY)
9T20	0925	MSX	0810 Carlisle to Warcop
7V00	0958	SX	0854 Carlisle to Severn Tunnel Junction
6E01	1107	SX	2325 Mossend to Healey Mills
6M12	1251	TO	0722 Elswick to Ellesmere Port (COY)
8E13	1520	SX	1310 Carlisle to Healey Mills
6E65	1654	SX	1322 Mossend to Healey Mills

Down

Code	Time at Appleby	Days	Train details
6M73	0742	SX	0345 Healey Mills to Carlisle
6S52	0844	MSX	0505 Winsford to Mossend (COY)
9T20	1150	MSX	1150 Appleby to Carlisle
6S52	1221	MO	0823 Winsford to Mossend (COY)
8P04	1343	SX	0540 Bescot to Carlisle
6S35	1850	TThO	1530 Burn Naze to Stevenston (COY)
6S98	1936	SX	0755 Severn Tunnel Junction to Mossend
8M64	1954	SX	1520 Healey Mills to Carlisle
8P28	2239	SX	1415 Bescot to Carlisle

(COY) = company train; other services are wagonload

THE WAGONLOAD LEGACY

Hump shunting at Temple Mills yard: the primary retarders catch a raft of six MXV wagons, loaded with scrap metal from Stratford Market, on 4 December 1980. The hump at Temple Mills remained in use until 1982, after which all traffic was flat-shunted from the south end.

Although not ranking as one of the major London yards, Acton yard took on greater importance in the 1970s when marshalling ceased at Brent (Cricklewood) on the London Midland Region and Norwood on the Southern Region. No 08486 shunts empty HTV hoppers at the west end of Acton yard on 8 August 1983. By that time Acton was handling mainly air-braked Speedlink traffic, together with residual vacuum-braked coal traffic for various concentration depots around London. The yard closed as a marshalling point in 1984.

Although the opening of new marshalling yards brought a welcome reduction in the number and complexity of short 'trip' workings between nearby yards in areas such as Carlisle and Teesside, many wagons still had to be shunted several times in the course of their journey. Where possible BR prescribed the composition of trunk wagonload trains in such a way as to make shunting easier. The table overleaf lists some sample formations for wagonload trains in North West England in 1978. In addition to sorting wagons by destination, it was often necessary to separate unfitted wagons (ie those without a continuous brake) from vacuum-

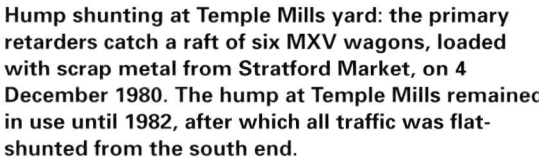

Left Classic Settle & Carlisle rail freight: No 40083 whistles north over Dandry Mire Viaduct, Garsdale, with a typically mixed consist for Carlisle yard on 5 September 1980. In the middle of the train are two air-braked hopper wagons, likely to be on their way to or from repairs.

braked wagons for the same destination in order to provide a 'fitted head', ie sufficient continuously braked wagons at the front of the train to maintain adequate brake force. However, personal observation from the period suggests that those formations were not always adhered to.

The inefficiencies of the wagonload network were compounded by the delays that often occurred at loading and discharge points. The National Coal Board had a particularly bad reputation for using railway-owned wagons as pithead storage bunkers, without paying any fee to the railway. A similar problem occurred at some ports and goods stations, where it suited the customer to delay loading or unloading.

RAIL FREIGHT: WAGONLOAD

Marshalling instructions for selected wagonload services calling at Warrington, 1978

7F23 1555 SX Barrow to Warrington Arpley
1 Warrington (fitted)
2 Carnforth
3 Warrington (unfitted)
At Carnforth: detach 2 and attach

7P08 0542 SX Bescot to Carlisle
1 Carlisle (fitted)
2 Warrington
3 Carlisle (unfitted)
At Warrington Walton Old Junction: detach 2 and attach

7F48 1415 SX Bescot to Warrington Walton Old Junction
1 Sandbach (tanks with barrier wagons)
2 Carlisle (fitted)
3 Warrington
4 Carlisle (unfitted)
At Crewe Basford Hall: detach 1

6O90 0320 MSX Carlisle to Eastleigh (7O90 from Warrington)
1 Eastleigh
2 Warminster
3 Severn Tunnel Junction
4 Warrington (including discharged flasks for Valley and Trawsfynydd)
5 Brake van (when flasks passing)
At Warrington Arpley: detach 4 and attach
At Severn Tunnel Junction: detach 3 and attach
At Westbury: detach 2

8G80 0600 SX Carlisle to Bescot
1 Penrhyndeudraeth (including barrier wagons)
2 Bescot Up (fitted)
3 Warrington
4 Bescot Up (unfitted)
5 Bescot Down
At Warrington Arpley: detach 3

7V30 0800 SX Carlisle to Severn Tunnel Junction
1 Blackburn
2 Warrington (including discharged flasks for Valley and Trawsfynydd)
3 Severn Tunnel Junction Down
4 Severn Tunnel Junction (including discharged flasks for Berkeley and Bridgwater)
At Blackburn: detach 1
At Warrington Arpley: detach 2 and attach

7A09 0934 SX Carlisle to Willesden
1 Willesden (fitted, including discharged flasks for Lydd, Leiston and Southminster)
2 Warrington
3 Willesden (unfitted)
At Warrington Arpley: detach 2 and attach

7G02 1840 SX Carlisle to Bescot
1 Bescot Up (fitted)
2 Warrington
3 Blackburn
4 Bescot Up (unfitted)
5 Bescot Down
At Blackburn: detach 3 and attach
At Warrington Arpley: detach 2 and attach

6S73 1100 SX Dover to Dundee (air-braked service)
1 Temple Mills (including Stewarts Lane)
2 Warrington
3 Dundee
4 Perth
5 Sighthill
6 Mossend
7 Carlisle
8 Bescot
9 Willesden
10 Tinsley
At Willesden: detach 1, 9 and 10, and attach
At Bescot: detach 8 and attach
At Warrington Walton Old Junction: detach 2, attach and leave:
1 Dundee
2 Perth
3 Sighthill
4 Lugton (Thursdays only)
5 Mossend
6 Carlisle
At Carlisle: detach 6 and attach
At Mossend: detach 3, 4 and 5
At Perth: detach 2

THE WAGONLOAD LEGACY

6M76 1605 SX Dundee to Bescot (air-braked service)
1. Kidderminster
2. Bescot
3. Warrington
4. Wigan
5. Carlisle

At Carlisle: detach 5 and attach
At Wigan North Western: detach 4
At Warrington Arpley: detach 3

7H11 1442 SX Edge Hill to Ashburys
1. Dover for continent (dual-braked)
2. Whitemoor (air-braked)
3. Ipswich (air-braked)
4. Dover (air-braked)

At Widnes: attach
At Warrington Arpley: attach and leave:
1. Dover for continent (dual-braked)
2. Dewsnap
3. Whitemoor (air-braked)
4. Ipswich (air-braked)
5. Dover (air-braked)

At Dewsnap: detach 2, 3 and 4

7M22 0850 SX Exeter to Warrington Walton Old Junction
1. Warrington (fitted, including loaded flasks for Sellafield)
2. Bescot
3. Kidderminster

At Kidderminster: detach 2 and 3
At Bescot: attach

8M89 0015 MX Healey Mills to Warrington Arpley
1. Warrington (fitted)
2. Ellesmere Port
3. Warrington (unfitted)

8M41 1330 SX Healey Mills to Warrington Arpley
1. Ellesmere Port (fitted)
2. Warrington
3. Ellesmere Port (unfitted)

6S78 2245 Llandeilo Junction to Mossend (air-braked service)
1. Westhoughton
2. Warrington
3. Blackburn
4. Mossend
5. Carlisle

At Warrington Walton Old Junction: detach 1 and 2 and attach
At Blackburn: detach 3 and attach
At Carlisle: detach 5 and attach

6M62 0006 MX March to Edge Hill (air-braked service)
1. Dewsnap
2. Widnes
3. Garston
4. Warrington

At Dewsnap: detach 1
At Warrington Arpley: detach 4
At Widnes: attach 2

7M49 0445 SX Margam to Warrington Walton Old Junction
1. Carlisle (fitted)
2. Warrington
3. Carlisle (unfitted)

6V93 0050 MSX Mossend to Severn Tunnel Junction
1. Blackburn
2. Warrington
3. Severn Tunnel Junction Down
4. Severn Tunnel Junction Up
5. Carlisle

At Carlisle: detach 5 and attach
At Blackburn: detach 1 and attach
At Warrington Arpley: detach 2 and attach
At Severn Tunnel Junction Up: detach 4

4M38 2120 SX Mossend to Willesden (air-braked service)
1. Plumstead
2. Luton
3. Acton
4. Willesden
5. Warrington

At Warrington Arpley: detach 5 and attach

7M81 0335 MO Severn Tunnel Junction to Warrington Walton Old Junction
1. Bescot Steel (fitted)
2. Bescot (fitted)
3. Wednesbury, Great Bridge and Wolverhampton (fitted)
4. Brierley Hill

RAIL FREIGHT: WAGONLOAD

5   Wednesbury, Great Bridge and Wolverhampton (unfitted)
6   Bescot (unfitted)
7   Bescot Steel (unfitted)
At Kingswinford Junction: detach 4
At Great Bridge or Wednesbury: detach 3 and 5

7M01 0855 SX Severn Tunnel Junction to Warrington Walton Old Junction
1   Warrington (fitted)
2   Croes Newydd
3   Warrington (unfitted)
At Croes Newydd: detach 2 and attach

7M46 2130 SX Severn Tunnel Junction to Warrington Walton Old Junction
1   Warrington (fitted)
2   Carlisle
3   Warrington (unfitted)

7F08 2240 SX Toton to Warrington Walton Old Junction
1   Warrington (fitted)
2   Stoke
3   Dewsnap (fitted)
4   Warrington (unfitted)
At Stoke: detach 2 and 3 and attach
At Grange Junction: attach

7V39 0027 MX Warrington Arpley to Exeter
1   Exeter (fitted)
2   Severn Tunnel Junction Up
3   Severn Tunnel Junction Down

8P36 0642 MSX Warrington Walton Old Junction to Workington
1   Workington (fitted)
2   Sellafield (loaded flasks)
3   Corkickle
4   Carnforth
5   Barrow
6   Workington (unfitted)
At Carnforth: detach 4 and 5 and attach
At Sellafield: detach 2 and attach
At Corkickle: detach 3

7P12 1428 SX Warrington Walton Old Junction to Carlisle
1   Carlisle (fitted)
2   Barrow
3   Carnforth
4   Workington
5   Carlisle (unfitted)
At Carnforth: detach 2 and 3 and attach
At Workington: detach 4 and attach

7P28 2113 SX Warrington Walton Old Junction to Carlisle
1   Carlisle (fitted)
2   Blackburn
3   Carlisle (unfitted)
At Blackburn: detach 2 and attach

7P20 2225 SX Warrington Walton Old Junction to Carlisle
1   Carlisle
At Blackburn: attach

6V86 2345 SX Warrington Arpley to Margam (air-braked service)
1   Swansea
2   Margam
3   Cardiff
4   Severn Tunnel Junction
At Cardiff: detach 3 and 4

4S48 2105 SX Willesden to Mossend (air-braked service)
1   Bathgate
2   Sighthill
3   Mossend
4   Warrington
At Rugby: attach to 2
At Warrington Walton Old Junction: detach 4 and attach

7P81 2225 FSX Willesden to Blackburn
1   Blackburn (fitted)
2   Carlisle (fitted)
3   Warrington (fitted, including loaded flasks for Sellafield)
4   Warrington (air braked)
5   Warrington (unfitted)
6   Carlisle (unfitted)
7   Blackburn (unfitted)
At Bletchley: attach Readers Digest traffic
At Warrington Walton Old Junction: detach 2 to 6 and attach

THE WAGONLOAD LEGACY

Still in two-tone green livery, Class 25 No D7558 stands at Stechford station, east of Birmingham, with a local trip freight on 11 June 1970.
Michael Mensing

The centre-cab Clayton Type 1s were associated mainly with Scotland, but some examples of the short-lived class could be found on light freight workings in North East England. No 8597 passes Newcastle station with a northbound local trip on 4 May 1971. The three Conflat wagons loaded with Land Rovers are an interesting element in the train.
J. H. Cooper-Smith

Class 40 No 365 passes Wood Green with the afternoon King's Cross Goods to Millerhill fully fitted freight on 4 November 1971. The train comprises mainly empty Insulfish vans.
J. H. Cooper-Smith

Single Class 20 haulage was not uncommon in the 1970s. No 20166 passes Stenson Junction with a partially fitted trip working from Toton to Burton on 7 March 1979, conveying loaded mineral wagons for local distribution, grain hoppers for the brewery trade and empty mgr hoppers for repair. *Michael Mensing*

One area where the Beeching recommendations had already taken effect by 1968 was the rationalisation of public goods terminals. Originally virtually every passenger station was accompanied by a goods yard, often with a separate area for coal-class traffic and a shed for goods requiring protection from the elements. This provision dated back to the time when road transport equated to the horse and cart and when it made sense to move goods as close as possible to their final destination by rail. Given the massive improvements to the road network that had taken place since the 1930s, the justification for keeping goods facilities at every station when overall volumes were in decline had become very weak.

A significant cull of station goods yards took place in the mid-1960s, as the accompanying list from the Midland main line illustrates. A similar decline in small private sidings took place, albeit spread over a longer period. The closure of goods yards and private sidings enabled BR to withdraw many of its slow and inefficient pick-up goods trains. The axe also fell on some locations that used to produce substantial wagonload volumes, such as the ports of Southampton and Liverpool. Overall, the thinning out of the network resulted in just 33% of BR's freight tonnage being moved by the wagonload in 1972.

Nevertheless, local trip workings still operated intensively around many towns and cities, as shown by the accompanying list of trip workings around Manchester in 1982. And traditional 'pick-up' operations held out for a surprisingly long time in some rural districts, even though they must have been heavy loss-makers on the BR balance sheet. In Norfolk, for example, BR operated a daily pick-up service on the Fakenham branch, calling at Wymondham, Dereham, North Elmham and

Closure dates for BR goods depots, Midland main line from London to Leicester (exclusive)

Mill Hill Broadway	1964	Leagrave	1984	Desborough	1968
Elstree	1967	Harlington	1967	Market Harborough	1979
Radlett	1968	Flitwick	1967	East Langton	1964
St Albans	1967	Ampthill	1959	Kibworth	1966
Harpenden	1964	Bedford	1971	Great Glen	1964
Chiltern Green	1967	Oakley	1963	Wigston	1966
Luton Crescent Road	1991	Sharnbrook	1964		
(still in use 2005 for stone traffic)		Irchester	1965	The dates refer to the withdrawal of public goods facilities. In some cases the sidings remained in use afterwards for specific customers.	
		Wellingborough	1980		
Luton Limbury Road	1968	Finedon	1964		
(then became coal concentration depot; still in use 2005 for stone traffic)		Burton Latimer	1964		
		Kettering	1980		
		Glendon	1964		

THE WAGONLOAD LEGACY

Above Class 37 No 6961 is pictured at New England yard, Peterborough, with a local trip freight on 20 March 1972. In the background is a busy BR freight terminal and National Carriers Depot, representing the kind of general merchandise traffic that within a few years would fall victim to road competition.
J. H. Cooper-Smith

Below Class 25 No 5290, still with its obsolete 'D' prefix, passes Charnock Richard, south of Euxton Junction, with an up mixed freight on 14 July 1972. The first part of the train is made up of BR-design 12-ton vans, which would soon be replaced by higher-capacity air-braked vans on key traffic flows.
Tom Heavyside

RAIL FREIGHT: WAGONLOAD

Heading north from Rannoch on 23 May 1973 is Class 27 No 5357 with a mixed freight bound for Fort William. The train includes three covered hopper wagons that would have been used to carry alumina. *J. H. Cooper-Smith*

Great Ryburgh. Frequent stops for shunting and for operating the unmanned level crossings on the branch meant that the trip could not be completed in a single shift; a second crew had to travel by road from Norwich to take care of the return journey. Not until 1980 was the service cut back from Fakenham to Great Ryburgh. Other rural freight-only outposts that remained open for general wagonload traffic in the 1970s were Newcastle Emlyn (closed 1973), Wimborne (closed 1977), Wadebridge (closed 1978), Fraserburgh (closed 1979), Louth (closed 1980), Forfar (closed 1982) and Meeth (closed 1982). Also worthy of mention are several passenger branches that retained a pick-up freight service into the 1970s, such as Whitland to Pembroke Dock, Middlesbrough to Whitby and the Cambrian Coast line to Pwllheli.

Above After BR decided to abandon the use of four-character headcodes, many indicator panels were set at '0O00' before being either plated over or removed. No 47485 takes the branch into Croes Newydd yard, Wrexham, with a mixed train from the Shrewsbury direction on 12 July 1976. *Tom Heavyside*

Below Class 08 shunters quietly disappeared from most parts of the railway network as many small sidings closed and as more and more terminals became accessible to main-line traction. Bridgwater still had two private sidings and a busy public freight terminal when 08149 was photographed on local trip duties on 26 June 1978. *Michael Mensing*

RAIL FREIGHT: WAGONLOAD

Manchester area freight trips, 1982

Location	Arr	Dep	Location	Arr	Dep
9T01/0T01			**9T11/0T11**		
Ashburys		0620	Manchester Victoria		0600
Ardwick Freight Terminal	0625	0810	Middleton Junction	0630	0700
Ardwick No 3	0815		Chadderton Coal Depot	0710	0730
Ardwick Freight Terminal		0905	Middleton Junction	0740	
Ashburys	0910	1005	CEGB sidings as required		
Ardwick Freight Terminal	1010		Middleton Junction		1145
Ardwick No 3			Chadderton Coal Depot	1150	1200
Ardwick British Fuels			Middleton Junction	1210	
Ardwick Freight Terminal		1325	**9T12/0T12**		
Ashburys	1330	1535	Middleton Junction		1230
Ardwick Freight Terminal	1540	1800	Windsor Bridge	1302	1340
Ashburys	1805	2230	Pendleton TW Ward	1350	1415
Ardwick Freight Terminal	2235		Agecroft CEGB/NCB	1420	1440
Ardwick No 3			Windsor Bridge	1455	1525
Ardwick British Fuels			Hope Street C&W	1530	1630
Ardwick Freight Terminal		0135	Windsor Bridge	1635	1830
Ashburys	0140	0230	Cox & Danks	1835	1900
Ardwick No 3	0235		Agecroft	1905	1915
Ardwick Freight Terminal			Windsor Bridge	1930	1940
Ardwick No 3		0415	Manchester Victoria	1950	
Ashburys	0420		**9T25/0T25**		
9T02/0T02			Guide Bridge		0640
Ashburys		0635	Ashburys	0655	0725
shunt yard			Beswick	0800	0850
Ashburys	0905	1000	Ashburys	0905	1015
Ashton Road	1010	1030	Beswick	1050	1110
Ashburys	1040		Park	1120	1225
shunt yard			Beswick	1140	1225
Ashburys		1410	Ashburys	1240	1250
Ardwick No 3	1415	1425	Guide Bridge	1305	
Kobo Coal Conc'n Depot	1435	1530	**9T28**		
Ardwick No 3	1540	1550	Dewsnap		0856
Ashburys	1555	1620	Ash Bridge	0922	0927
Ashton Road	1630	1635	Reddish South	0932	0958
Ashburys	1645	1750	Stockport NCB	1014	1057
Ashton Road	1800	2045	Longsight	1119	1204
Ashburys	2055		Ardwick No 1	1214	1224
9T10/0T10			Dewsnap	1244	1324
Buxton Diesel Depot		1055	Ashburys	1339	1420
Higher Buxton	1117		Dewsnap	1435	
Hindlow			**9T29**		
Briggs Sidings		1725	Dewsnap		0950
Buxton Diesel Depot	1800				

THE WAGONLOAD LEGACY

Location	Arr	Dep	Location	Arr	Dep
either Partington	1048	1132	Buxton	1540	1615
or Glazebrook	1055	1125	Briggs Sidings	1640	1715
Dewsnap	1224	1345	Peak Forest	1800	1820
Northenden	1410	1445	Dewsnap	1920	2040
Dewsnap	1540		Peak Forest	2145	2200
			Buxton Diesel Depot	2225	
9T30			**0T35**		
Dewsnap		0620	Buxton Diesel Depot		1645
Trafford Park	0654	0740	Tunstead	1716	
Ashburys	0820	0845	bank loaded trains as required		
Dewsnap	0900	1017	Peak Forest		2305
Trafford Park	1051	1145	Buxton Diesel Depot	2332	
Dewsnap	1220	1525	**0T36**		
Trafford Park	1559	1715	Buxton Diesel Depot		0405
Ashburys	1744	1814	Tunstead	0428	
Dewsnap	1829	1946	Peak Forest and Topley Pike as required		
Trafford Park	2020	2050	also bank loaded trains as required		
Dewsnap	2125		Peak Forest		2308
0T33/6T33/9T33			Buxton Diesel Depot	2335	
Buxton Diesel Depot		1345	**9T37**		
Peak Forest	1412	1440	Earles Sidings		1840
Earles Sidings	1530		Dewsnap	1955	
Edale, Bamford and Grindleford as required			**9T38**		
Earles Sidings		1920	Dewsnap		0030
Peak Forest	2020	2035	Earles Sidings	0147	
Buxton Diesel Depot	2100		**9T44/0T44**		
9T34/0T34			Newton Heath Depot		0601
Buxton Diesel Depot		0825	Ashburys	0620	0650
Peak Forest	0900	0930	Skew Bridge	0710	0725
Higher Buxton	1005	1020	Ashburys	0740	0802
Peak Forest	1050	1120	Dewsnap	0822	0901
Dewsnap	1220	1340	Ashburys	0921	1001
Peak Forest	1450	1510			

The daily Ashburys to Hindlow trip working passes New Mills South Junction behind No 40184 on 28 October 1982. The load includes CHV covered hoppers and OWV open wagons returning to Hindlow for lime traffic.

RAIL FREIGHT: WAGONLOAD

Location	Arr	Dep	Location	Arr	Dep
Dewsnap	1016	1055	**9T49/0T49**		
Ashburys	1115	1140	Newton Heath Depot		0713
Manchester Victoria	1200	1232	Ashburys (MWFO)	0730	0800
Red Bank	1240	1250	Middleton Junction	0827	0859
Dewsnap	1327	1404	Dewsnap	0938	1033
Ashburys	1424	1525	Ashburys	1043	1106
Dewsnap	1545	1625	Castleton	1140	
Ashburys	1640	1703	Heywood as required		
Dewsnap	1723	1802	Castleton		1248
Ashburys	1822	1831	Dewsnap	1339	1349
Newton Heath Depot	1846	2325	Newton Heath Depot	1413	
Skew Bridge	2330	0001	**8T53/0T53**		
Dewsnap	0025	0105	Newton Heath Depot		0742
Ashburys	0125	0255	Ashburys	0800	0830
Dewsnap	0315	0355	Windsor Bridge	0852	0933
Ashburys	0415	0445	Bolton	0958	
Newton Heath Depot	0500		shunt NCL and Trinity Street		
6T54/9T54/9T46			Bolton		1155
Newton Heath Depot		0555	Windsor Bridge	1218	1248
Ashburys	0620	0650	Brindle Heath	1255	1321
Horwich	0820	0950	Windsor Bridge	1329	1359
Dewsnap	1128	1223	Dewsnap	1430	1440
Horwich	1359	1529	Newton Heath Depot	1502	
Ashburys	1646	1711	**8T75**		
Dewsnap	1728	1738	Walton Old Junction		0950
Newton Heath Depot	1802		Glazebrook	1045	1105
			Warrington Central	1125	1155
			Glazebrook	1215	1235
			Arpley	1340	

The Cambrian Coast line still offered the anachronistic sight of pick-up goods trains until well into the 1970s. The main traffics carried were explosives from Cooke's at Penrhyndeudraeth and coal to Tywyn, Porthmadog and Pwllheli. On 26 September 1978 No 25325 arrives at Harlech with one empty CXV gunpowder van for Penrhyndeudraeth, an MCO wagon carrying coal from Gwaun-cae-Gurwen to Porthmadog and an MCV wagon carrying coal from Gwaun-cae-Gurwen to Pwllheli.

THE WAGONLOAD LEGACY

No 25149 shunts chemical tanks for Albright & Wilson on the short branch to Preston Street goods, Whitehaven, on 21 July 1979. The wooden signal arm is an interesting relic. *Tom Heavyside*

Imported fruit for the Cadbury Schweppes factory at Histon completed its journey on the daily Fen Drayton sand train, which called at Histon on its return leg to detach and attach wagons. No 37036 comes off the Fen Drayton branch at Chesterton Junction on 1 May 1980, with one empty ferry van from Histon and HTV wagons conveying sand for King's Cross.

Nos 25048 and 25207 approach Bodmin Road station with 7A19, the 1810 St Blazey to Acton, on 11 June 1980. The load comprises bagged china clay in ferry vans (the second of which is a British-registered van), bulk china clay in tarpaulined OWV open wagons, bagged china clay in a VVV van and – out of sight – a single empty MCV mineral wagon.

RAIL FREIGHT: WAGONLOAD

No 76001, one of the few Woodhead electrics not equipped for multiple working, crosses Dinting Viaduct with a special freight from Warrington to Tinsley on 17 September 1980. The formation includes a VVV van carrying oil drums from Liverpool to Norwich, several different wagon types loaded with wooden sleepers, and half a dozen CGO grain hopper wagons.

Passing the fine array of semaphore signals at Barrow Hill are Nos 20142 and 20183 in charge of 8E16, the 0930 Bescot to Tinsley wagonload train, on 27 July 1981.

BR maintained a nationwide collection and delivery service for wagonload goods traffic in the 1970s by running longer-distance road connections to and from a network of principal goods depots, at most of which BR also provided cranage for heavy loads. In a few locations BR built a new depot, such as Sheffield Freight Terminal, which replaced a number of smaller goods yards in the Sheffield area. But in most cases the overall reduction in wagonload volumes made it possible for BR to concentrate the remaining traffic on an existing centrally located terminal.

By February 1981 the number of BR goods stations with cranage and collection and delivery facilities for steel and other heavy loads had fallen to 74, as listed in the accompanying table. In some parts of the country BR would collect and deliver over long distances – for example, Aberystwyth customers were served from the BR railhead at Shrewsbury, Pwllheli customers from Llandudno Junction, and Kettering customers from Luton.

For traffic where the customer took care of the handling and delivery, BR retained a larger number of unstaffed terminals, often referred to as 'public delivery sidings'. These terminals were spread rather unevenly across the country. Some survived longer than they might otherwise have done because they handled a specific traffic flow, such as bitumen at Skipton and chemicals for Ciba-Geigy at Whittlesford. A number of former station goods depots in South East England became dedicated terminals for roadstone traffic.

THE WAGONLOAD LEGACY

BR freight depots with cranage, February 1981

Location	Max lift (tonnes)	Location	Max lift (tonnes)	Location	Max lift (tonnes)
Aberdeen Guild Street	15	Great Bridge	25	St Neots	8
Banbury	10	Grimsby Holles Street	9	Scunthorpe	21
Barking Ripple Lane	15	Heysham	12	Sheffield Freight Terminal	35
Barnstaple	5	Holyhead	18	Shrewsbury Castle Foregate	10
Basingstoke	15	Hull Central	18	Southampton Bevois Park	15
Birkenhead Morpeth Dock	8	Inverness	11	Spalding	7
Birmingham Landor Street	11	Ipswich	8	Stranraer Harbour	10
Bolton Halliwell	11	Kidderminster	8	Sunderland Monkwearmouth	15
Bridgwater	56	Kirkcaldy	11	Swansea Hafod	15
Brierley Hill	20	Leeds Whitehall Road	20	Thurso	10
Bury St Edmunds	10	Leicester Nedham Street	20	Tilbury Riverside	9
Cambridge Coalfields	9	Leith South	15	Valley	56
Carlisle London Road	13	Liverpool Canada Dock	40	Walsall Tasker Street	15
Coventry	11	Llandudno Junction	10	Warrington Central	11
Derby St Mary's	11	London Park Royal	30	Weaverthorpe	7
Diss	8	London Stratford LIFT	7	Wednesbury Central	20
Doncaster Central	10	Longport	15	Wellington (Salop)	11
Dundee West	11	Manchester Ardwick West	11	Wigan North Western	11
Elgin East	11	Middlesbrough	15	Wolverhampton Steel Terminal	40
Falkirk Grahamston	11	Newhaven Harbour	12	Worksop	15
Fishguard Harbour	25	Norwich Thorpe	15	Wrexham Watery Road	8
Fort William	4	Poole	11	Yarmouth Vauxhall	8
Gateshead Tyneside CFD	20	Port Glasgow Bogston	11		
Glasgow High Street	25	Portsmouth Fratton	15		
Gloucester Llanthony	15	Redhill	15		
Goole	8	Rochester	15		

In the early 1980s BR still routed substantial tonnages of wagonload freight between the Midlands and the east side of London via Whitemoor and Temple Mills yards. No 31189 passes Whittlesford with a well-loaded 8J93 from Whitemoor to Temple Mills on 5 June 1981. The station goods yard was busy at that time with chemicals for Ciba-Geigy, soon to be transferred to the company's new private siding at Duxford.

RAIL FREIGHT: WAGONLOAD

One of the last areas to witness a virtually all-stations wagonload service was the Far North line from Inverness to Wick and Thurso, where even small stations such as Tain, Ardgay and Golspie were still open for goods in February 1981. The North of Scotland was the last outpost for two further relict operations until the early 1980s: wagonloads of fish, which were attached to passenger trains from Wick to Inverness and from Inverness to Aberdeen; and mixed passenger and freight trains on the Kyle of Lochalsh and Mallaig branches. The oil traffic to Mallaig continued to travel by mixed train from Fort William until 1987.

The Beeching vision for rescuing BR's wagonload traffic had foreseen three possible solutions for individual flows. The heaviest and most regular movements could be converted to trainload operation; smaller consignments between major centres could form the basis of a new liner train network; and the least remunerative traffic would be abandoned.

The traffic most suited to trainload operation was coal. BR succeeded in increasing the proportion of coal carried by the trainload significantly during the late 1960s and 1970s, mainly due to the opening of new power stations that were designed to be fed by 'merry-go-round' (mgr) trainloads. However, coal for domestic consumption still moved by the wagonload; indeed, in the early 1980s coal was the last traffic that remained on some parts of the wagonload network.

The last outpost for BR's 'blue spot' Insulfish vans was the North of Scotland, where BR carried fish from Wick to Aberdeen on scheduled passenger trains. Nos 26026 and 26046 prepare to depart from Georgemas Junction with the afternoon combined train from Wick and Thurso to Inverness on 24 September 1980, with one Insulfish van in the formation and another – presumably empty – waiting in the siding.

In 1976 the first train of the day to Kyle of Lochalsh was a mixed passenger, parcels and freight working. It is pictured just after arrival at the terminus on 17 August, hauled by No 26038, with one passenger coach, an assortment of parcels coaches and one empty Lowmac wagon. The sidings on the left are filled with stored wagons.

THE WAGONLOAD LEGACY

Invergordon was a busy location for rail freight in the early 1980s, with private sidings for British Aluminium, Invergordon Distillery and M. K. Shand as well as a BR public freight terminal. On 20 March 1981 No 26042 arrives with the morning passenger train to Inverness, while No 40167 waits on the down line with one FBB flat wagon carrying an empty whisky tank from Glasgow High Street to Invergordon Distillery and a mixture of cement, open and covered hopper wagons for the other terminals.

The Forfar branch produced healthy volumes of wagonload freight traffic until shortly before its closure in June 1982. No 27023 shunts Forfar goods yard before returning to Perth with the daily 8P04 trip working on 23 March 1981. The traffic on that occasion included seed potatoes from Forfar to Coventry and Ely and fertiliser from France to Forfar. The open wagon next to the locomotive was to be loaded with timber, while the second brake-van was kindly provided by BR for members of the Cambridge University Railway Club.

Having been redeployed from its Edinburgh-Glasgow push-pull duties, No 27101 pulls out of Dumfries yard with a uniform rake of VWV vans for Carlisle on 24 August 1981.

Above Traffic to and from the Derwent Valley Light Railway (DVLR) at Foss Islands produced regular trip workings to and from Dringhouses yard. No 08559 has just passed through York station on 11 August 1981 with a mixed rake of wagons from the DVLR including CHP covered hoppers, VVV vans and HKV hoppers.

Left One of the most photogenic long-distance wagonload services in the early 1980s was 6S98, the 0755 fully-fitted service from Severn Tunnel Junction to Mossend. No 47230 heads 6S98 past Pontrilas on 13 April 1982, with a typically wide variety of rolling-stock including coal hoppers, minerals, oil tanks, vans and an assortment of hooded steel coil carriers.

THE WAGONLOAD LEGACY

No 31302 passes Ferryhill with the afternoon wagonload service from Tyne Yard to Tees Yard on 8 June 1982. The formation includes empty bogie bolster wagons, anhydrous ammonia tanks and loaded coal hoppers.

Opportunities to transfer other wagonload flows to trainload operation in the 1960s and 1970s were limited. The volume of traffic moving between any given pair of locations was rarely large or stable enough to justify trainload operation – a problem that the railway has continued to face in more recent times. Often the best solution was to use a combination of block working and wagonload feeder services, as illustrated by the table overleaf for Anglo-Scottish grain traffic. Unfortunately the costs of operating the various trip workings in rural Yorkshire, Lincolnshire and Cambridgeshire were substantial.

A compromise solution for those wagonload flows that were judged to be worth retaining but could not produce trainload volumes was the air-braked Speedlink network, discussed in greater detail in the next section of this book. Although Speedlink did not come into being until the 1970s, it put into practice one of Beeching's aims: to reduce the amount of intermediate shunting incurred by wagonload traffic and extend the length of the trunk haul as far as possible.

BR's attempts to transfer general merchandise traffic to liner trains achieved only limited success. Beeching had proposed a national network of liner train routes, serving about 50 railheads. Some of those railheads were to be very close to each other, such as Coventry and Birmingham. Traffic would be carried in 10ft, 20ft and 30ft containers and loaded on a new generation of air-braked flat wagons capable of travelling at 75mph. As things turned out, the liner train concept developed successfully into the Freightliner network that exists today, but many of the proposed regional terminals such as Chester, Oxford and Norwich were never built, and the network as a whole soon

RAIL FREIGHT: WAGONLOAD

Feeder services for grain traffic from Eastern Region to Scotland, 1978

Forwarding point	Service	
Ancaster	6T21	1227 SX to Sleaford
	9D86	0505 MSX Whitemoor to Doncaster (from Sleaford)
	8D86	0515 SO Whitemoor to Doncaster (from Sleaford)
Dunnington	Derwent Valley Railway to Foss Islands	
	9K09	1145 SO Foss Islands to Dringhouses
	9K09	1630 SX Foss Islands to Dringhouses
Gainsborough Lea Road	7T06	0935 MWFO to Doncaster
Grantham	8J06	1535 SX to Doncaster
Grimsby	7J66	1802 SX to Tinsley (detach Doncaster)
Immingham	9T80	1452 SX to Grimsby West Marsh
	7J66	1802 SX Grimsby to Tinsley (detach Doncaster)
Knapton	8K10	0730 SX Scarborough to Dringhouses (from Knapton)
Louth	9T93	1148 MWFO to Grimsby West Marsh
	7J66	1802 SX Grimsby to Tinsley (detach Doncaster)
Royston	7T43	1415 SX to Letchworth
	7P06	1832 SX Welwyn GC to Whitemoor (from Letchworth)
Sandy	7Y50	1400 SX Sandy to Peterborough West
	7P02	2355 SX Peterborough West to Whitemoor
Tuxford	Trip as required to Mansfield Concentration Sidings	
	8J31	2116 SX Mansfield CS to Tinsley
	8D42	0335 MX Tinsley to Doncaster
Trunk services		
9D86	0550 MSX Whitemoor to Doncaster	
8D86	0515 SO Whitemoor to Doncaster	
8D86	0717 MO Whitemoor to Doncaster	
6S40	1445 SX Doncaster to Burghead (attaches at York)	
6S43	1445 SX Doncaster to Dufftown (attaches at York)	
6S43	1445 SX Doncaster to Muir of Ord (attaches at York)	

became geared to deep-sea containers rather than domestic movements.

The various changes outlined above led to a progressive decline in the wagonload freight network. By the late 1970s some wagonload trains carried less true revenue-earning freight than departmental traffic such as ballast, sleepers, diesel fuel and other materials used by the railway itself. Those materials travelled 'free on rail' and BR had little incentive to make economies; elderly and unkempt departmental wagons were a common sight languishing in sidings dotted around the network.

BR's efforts to phase out traditional wagonload operations reached a milestone in May 1983 when the network closed to all traffic except coal and scrap metal. Customers with other types of freight then had three options: they could switch to using air-braked wagons on the Speedlink network, run their traffic in full trainloads, or abandon rail altogether. Often the third option was the most realistic. For coal and scrap metal, BR gave its customers a further 12 months before withdrawing the traditional wagonload service. However, even then it was not quite the end: in North East England some trip workings still conveyed scrap metal in vacuum-braked wagons alongside air-braked stock as late as 1987.

THE WAGONLOAD LEGACY

Long after the planned withdrawal of vacuum-braked stock on all except specific trainload services, a mixed rake of vacuum-braked MDV/MDW scrap wagons and one air-braked TTB tank wagon is pictured at Dunston on 17 July 1986, forming the daily local trip working from Tyne Yard to Hexham. The motive power is No 31227. The scrap metal was destined for Teesside and the tank wagon was conveying resin from Duxford to Hexham.

Tees Yard

Tees Yard was the busiest of the hump marshalling yards built under the 1955 Modernisation Plan, with the capacity to handle 7,000 wagons daily. It revolutionised wagonload freight on Teesside, replacing not only the six small Newport yards on the same site but also the outlying yards at Stockton, Haverton Hill, Port Clarence and Middlesbrough. Unlike some other Modernisation Plan yards such as Carlisle and Whitemoor, which were built on green-field sites and acted mainly as intermediate marshalling points for long-distance traffic, Tees Yard was situated in a major industrial area and much of its traffic would be travelling to or from local terminals, especially those connected with the steel and chemical industries.

The chosen location for Tees Yard was a 200-acre site on the south bank of the Tees, partly on existing railway land and partly on reclaimed marshland. Preparatory work included the diversion of the Middlesbrough to Saltburn line around its southern edge and the re-routeing of Stainsby Beck, a tributary of the River Tees. When completed the yard would contain some 66 miles of track, and the layout would be 95 tracks wide at its broadest point. It stretched from milepost 11¼ at Thornaby station to milepost 14 at Newport East Junction.

Construction of the yard began in 1959. Its official opening took place in May 1963 in the presence of the Chairman and Managing Director of the Dorman Long Steel Company – a clear indication of the yard's intended role. But the tonnages handled at Tees never quite lived up to expectations: between 1959 and 1963 the total rail freight to and from Teesside had fallen from 9 million tons to less than 6 million tons, as competition from road transport began to bite and as the local industries changed their transport requirements. In practice the yard never handled more than 6,000 wagons a day.

Because of the large size of Tees Yard, it comprised separate down and up yards, each with its own mechanised hump. On the down side there were 12 reception lines, 42 primary sorting sidings, 10 secondary sorting sidings and 12 departure and staging sidings. The up yard consisted of 12 reception lines, 43 primary sorting sidings (including one dead-end siding) and 14 departure and staging sidings. At the tail end of each set of departure sidings were the inclined 'van kip' sidings, from where a brake-van would roll down on to the back of each departing train. There were two pairs of through goods lines: one pair flanked the yard with the down line on the north side and the up line on the south side, and the other pair ran through the middle of the yard. The up and down main lines both skirted the south side of the yard.

Shunting operations in Tees Yard were controlled from the up and down towers. The down tower also contained a panel for the main line between Middlesbrough West and Bowesfield. The

The inclined 'van kip' provided a simple method of attaching a brake-van to the rear of each departing train. Passing the up yard kip on 19 March 1981 is No 40192 with a lightly loaded Speedlink trip working, conveying one BKB wagon with coil from South Bank to Wolverhampton and one IWB ferry van with plate from South Bank to Basel.

hump operators in each tower had the highly skilled job of controlling the flow of wagons into the sorting sidings as they rolled off the hump. They had to regulate the speed of each wagon or group of wagons so that it rolled far enough along the siding but not too far. The operator achieved this by selecting one of six settings on the secondary retarders, depending on his assessment of the occupation level of the siding, the curvature of the siding, the condition of the wagon, and the strength and direction of the wind. If a wagon stopped too soon, then time would have to be spent shunting it with a pilot locomotive; if it rolled too far, it could cause a collision and, possibly, a derailment.

The benefit of hump shunting was the reduced time taken to sort a train comprising wagons for half a dozen or more different destinations. If the hump pilot locomotive pushed its train on to the hump at walking pace, then the 'cuts' of wagons would roll down at sufficient intervals to allow the points to change between each 'cut', and a typical train could be sorted in about 15 minutes. To perform the same task by flat shunting would take much longer.

Arriving trains were directed to either up or down reception sidings depending on the nature and destination of their load. The down yard focused mainly on traffic destined for Teesside, while the up yard tended to handle traffic for other parts of the country. Most main-line arrivals at Tees were therefore routed into the down receptions; any wagons for onward trunk services would need to be transferred by a pilot locomotive to the up yard. Trip workings from terminals on and around Teesside were normally routed into the up receptions. Permanent way trains, including anything up to ten weekend engineering trains, were marshalled in the down yard.

As far as possible each siding in the primary yards was allocated to a specific destination and, in some cases, traffic type. During the transition period from vacuum-braked to air-braked operation, some destinations had one siding for vacuum-braked (and unfitted) wagons and another for air-braked wagons. Preferential treatment was given to air-braked wagons for Speedlink services, where any late running could have serious consequences. The timings of Speedlink trains were often tight: for example, the afternoon service from Haverton Hill to Harwich was allowed only 40 minutes at Tees Yard to detach and attach traffic and to reverse direction.

The wagons for departing trains were assembled as far as possible in the main sorting sidings. Yard staff would 'short couple' the wagons so that the couplings were tight enough to prevent jerking when the train started moving. A pilot locomotive would often need to rearrange the wagons in order to comply with marshalling instructions, including the provision of a vacuum-braked 'fitted head' on partially braked trains and the positioning of certain very long or heavy wagons at the head of the formation. Each train would then be drawn out into the departure sidings ready for the

THE WAGONLOAD LEGACY

An internal view of the down control tower, overlooking the down yard, and a trio of HTO hopper wagons passing over the up yard retarders on 12 September 1980.

attachment of the main-line locomotive and, if necessary, brake-van.

Although the yard staff were essentially focused on operations, they often had to make decisions based on business criteria. In the customer's eyes any time that his wagon spent in the marshalling yard was wasted time; similarly it was important to maintain an adequate flow of empty wagons to loading points. If necessary the regular programme of trunk departures could be supplemented by specials, ideally by making use of what would otherwise have been a light engine movement.

The volumes handled at Tees increased in the mid-1960s, but then began to fall as the effects of the Beeching Report took their toll. More and more traffic was being moved in full trainloads and many small private sidings and goods depots were closed. Rationalisation in the coal, steel and chemical industries meant that there was no longer a need for complex movements of coal and coke from numerous Durham pits to Teesside blast furnaces, foundries and chemical plants.

Nevertheless, even in the late 1970s the yard still supported a substantial programme of local trip workings, as listed in the table overleaf. Some of these workings followed a set route, while others could be directed to whichever terminals needed servicing at any given time. Flexibility was essential to make the best use of resources; sometimes it was possible for an engine and crew to work five or six successive trips within a single turn.

RAIL FREIGHT: WAGONLOAD

Tees Yard trips, 1979

Location	Arr	Dep
9P65 MX		
Tees Yard	2355	0020
as required		
9P96/6K96		
Tees Yard	0410	0430
Lackenby	0500	0530
Hartlepool South Wks	0630	0745
Lackenby	0845	0915
Tees Yard	0945	
9P60 MO		
Tees Yard	0505	0530
as required		
9P16/6K16		
Tees Yard	0505	0530
Lackenby	0600	0630
Skinningrove	0735	0855
Lackenby	1000	1030
Tees Yard	1100	
9P66		
Tees Yard	0546	0611
as required		
9P70		
Tees Yard	0550	0615
Middlesbrough area	0625	0655
Tees Yard	0705	0745
Grangetown area	0815	0845
Tees Yard	0915	1045
Grangetown area	1115	1145
Tees Yard	1215	
9P79		
Tees Yard	0635	0700
as required		
9P64 (WO)		
Tees Yard	0715	0730
Battersby (run round)		
Sleights		
Castleton		

Location	Arr	Dep
Battersby (run round)		
Tees Yard	1402	
9P73		
Tees Yard	0715	0740
Grangetown area	0810	0840
Tees Yard	0910	1040
Grangetown area	1110	1140
Tees Yard	1210	1250
South Bank area	1310	1340
Tees Yard	1400	
9P76		
Tees Yard	0735	0800
Stockton*	0820	0925
Tees Yard	0945	1115
Haverton Hill area	1150	1220
Tees Yard	1255	
*including Watson and Laverick coal depots		
9P69 (TThO)		
Tees Yard	0705	0730
Redcar		
Saltburn		
Brotton		
Carlin How		1235
Tees Yard	1352	
9P69 (MWFO)		
Tees Yard	0805	0830
Carlin How	0945	1015
Tees Yard	1130	1145
Carlin How	1245	1300
Tees Yard	1415	
9P80 (MWFO)		
Tees Yard	0839	0900
Bedale		
Leyburn	1050	1150
Redmire		
Leyburn		
Bedale		
Tees Yard	1506	

THE WAGONLOAD LEGACY

Location	Arr	Dep	Location	Arr	Dep
9P97/6K97			Tees Yard	1655	1810
Tees Yard	1110	1130	Haverton Hill area	1845	1915
Lackenby	1200	1230	Tees Yard	1950	
Hartlepool South Wks	1330	1445			
Lackenby	1545	1615	**9P86 (SO)**		
Tees Yard	1645		Tees Yard	1415	1440
			as required		
9P82					
Tees Yard			**9P08**		
Stockton area			Middlesbrough Yard		1320
Tees Yard			Tees Yard	1335	1400
Eaglescliffe area			Whitehouse	1420	1630
Tees Yard			Middlesbrough Yard	1645	
Eaglescliffe area			Tees Yard		
Tees Yard			Middlesbrough Yard	2030	
9P61			**9P84**		
Tees Yard	1205	1230	Tees Yard	1235	1300
Carlin How	1345	1415	as required		
Tees Yard	1530	1545			
Carlin How	1645	1700	**9P83**		
Tees Yard	1815		Tees Yard	1315	1340
			Middlesbrough area	1350	1420
9P76 (SO)			Tees Yard	1430	1510
Tees Yard	0735	0800	Haverton Hill area	1545	1615
Grangetown area	0830	0900	Tees Yard	1650	1820
Tees Yard	0930	1055	Grangetown area	1850	1920
Haverton Hill area	1130	1200	Tees Yard	1950	
Tees Yard	1235	1250			
Grangetown area	1310	1325	**9P86**		
Tees Yard	1355		Tees Yard	1526	1551
			as required		
9P82 (SO)					
Tees Yard	1135	1200	**9P18/6K18**		
South Bank area	1220	1250	Tees Yard	1705	1750
Tees Yard	1310	1350	Lackenby	1800	1830
Grangetown area	1410	1440	Skinningrove	1935	2055
Tees Yard	1510	1640	Lackenby	2200	2230
Grangetown area	1710	1740	Tees Yard	2300	
Tees Yard	1810				
			9P94		
9P83 (SO)			Tees Yard	2126	2151
Tees Yard	1315	1340	as required		
Grangetown area	1410	1440			
Tees Yard	1510	1550	All trains run SX unless otherwise noted		
Grangetown area	1620	1635			

RAIL FREIGHT: WAGONLOAD

Above No 08770 performs pilot duty in the down yard on 12 September 1980. By this time Tees was operating well below its capacity; many of the wagons visible in this photograph were in short- or long-term storage.

Below No 08502 shunts the last of a batch of HTO hoppers from Fishburn coke works over the up hump on 24 March 1982. Soon the hump would be closed and all remaining wagonload traffic transferred to the down yard.

Above No 47141 snakes out of the up yard on 25 May 1982 with 6C83, the 1605 Haverton Hill to Parkeston trunk Speedlink service. Only the first wagon in the train, a VTG-owned IPB van, was destined for the train ferry to Zeebrugge.

Below The early evening was a busy time for Tees Yard staff, with several tightly timed Speedlink departures. No 47309 leaves the up yard with 6O49, the 1750 train to Eastleigh, on 25 May 1982. The load comprises two TTA tanks with methanol from Haverton Hill to Eastleigh, two VCA vans in BR departmental use from Thornaby to Crewe, one BKB steel wagon with coil from Lackenby to Wolverhampton, and one VCA van in BR departmental use from Thornaby to York.

However, by 1979 Tees Yard was operating at less than a quarter of its design capacity. It was obvious that rationalisation would take place sooner or later. The first substantial cutback was the closure of the up reception sidings and hump in 1982, leaving a single-ended up yard shunted from the west end. The up hump was targeted first because it had seen heavier use and its retarders were becoming life-expired; because of the track layout it was also easier for BR to transfer traffic from the up to the down yard than vice versa.

The decline of the traditional wagonload freight network meant that even the remaining down hump was soon under-utilised. Speedlink traffic tended to involve larger numbers of wagons moving to a single destination and it was more efficient to shunt them on the flat. With fewer than 1,000 wagons passing through the yard each day, it was decided to close the down hump and reception sidings in 1985. The two flat yards that remained, comprising approximately 80 single-ended sidings, were more than ample for the foreseeable needs of Speedlink.

The end of Speedlink in 1991 might well have signalled the final demise of Tees Yard. Much less-than-trainload traffic was lost and the surviving flows were worked as block loads between terminals wherever possible. However, shunting was still necessary where trunk trains carried traffic to or from more than one terminal at each end of their route. Railfreight Distribution routed two trunk trains via Tees Yard: a chemicals train to Bescot, which conveyed carbon dioxide from Haverton Hill and chlorine from Wilton, and a European service, which originated at Crewe and called at Tees, Selby and Scunthorpe before returning to Bescot with ferry wagons for mainland Europe. It continued to operate trip workings between Tees and several local terminals, including Haverton Hill, Wilton, Tees Dock, Middlesbrough, Hartlepool, Thrislington and Ferryhill. And, even if no shunting were necessary, Tees Yard would retain a role for staging wagons and changing locomotives and crews, especially given the proximity of Thornaby traction depot. Several trainload flows of steel, limestone, cement and oil continued to call at Tees, in some cases detaching or attaching traffic despite their 'trainload' label.

At the time of writing the remnants of Tees Yard still handle revenue-earning freight traffic, even though the days of the busy hump yard are a distant memory. Among the timetabled services using the yard in 2005 were trains carrying containerised chemicals from Tees Dock to Workington, aluminium ingots from Lynemouth to Newport, limestone and lime from Hardendale and Shap to Corus Teesside (Lackenby/Redcar), and various flows of steel to and from Lackenby, Middlesbrough, Hartlepool and Skinningrove.

The decline of a station goods yard: Cambridge Coalfields, 1978-81

The BR goods terminal known as Cambridge Coalfields was an interesting example of its type as it continued to handle a wide range of wagonload freight traffic throughout the 1970s and even into the early 1980s. The yard was located adjacent to the south end of Cambridge passenger station. It consisted of two dead-end sidings with road access between them and was equipped with a 9-ton-capacity mobile crane. The traffic received there by rail was distributed by road throughout Cambridgeshire and as far afield as Spalding.

Wagons destined for Coalfields would be tripped there from Cambridge sorting sidings by one of the resident Class 08 pilot engines, usually in the early hours of the morning. A second visit would then be made in the evening to collect any outgoing wagons. The Class 08 would also serve other terminals in the immediate Cambridge area, including the Charringtons and Co-op coal concentration depots and the Esso oil terminal at Coldham's Lane. Cambridge sorting sidings were served by wagonload freight services running between Temple Mills and Whitemoor marshalling yards, plus in later years a Speedlink trip working between Duxford and Whitemoor.

The table on pages 41-42 gives a summary of goods consignments handled at Cambridge Coalfields during three eight-week periods in

A flurry of shunting activity at the south end of Cambridge station on 8 October 1980, as No 08863 manoeuvres a rake of BRVs in Coalfields goods yard and sister locomotive No 08862 makes its way to Charringtons coal depot.

THE WAGONLOAD LEGACY

No 37099 arrives at Cambridge sorting sidings on 8 June 1981 with 8J93, the afternoon wagonload service from Whitemoor to Temple Mills. The load includes MCV mineral wagons with scrap metal from Shipley to Sheerness, a CHV covered hopper wagon for Harlow Mill, sheeted KRV and KSV coil wagons from Scunthorpe to Rochester, HTV coal hoppers for Plumstead, and HTO coal hoppers for Colchester Hythe. The train will resume its journey after collecting any southbound traffic from Coalfields goods depot and other terminals in the Cambridge area.

1979. The information is based on personal observations made every weekday during each period. The overall wagon totals are distorted by the bulk deliveries of steel coil and military vehicles recorded during the second and third periods. The general picture in 1979 was in fact one of steady decline, a process that continued into the early 1980s as the various flows were lost or transferred to road transport.

A large proportion of the traffic handled at Cambridge Coalfields was military in nature. It included regular outgoing consignments of containers to the Central Ordnance Depot at Donnington, loaded mainly on BRV Borail wagons but with some air-braked PFB and SPA wagons appearing from late 1979 onwards. Military vehicles of various types were received and dispatched on a combination of railway-owned OLV low-sided wagons, BRV Borail wagons and privately owned PFB and PFV flat wagons. An unusual type of military traffic was the occasional dispatch of Morris Minor and Mini cars to the government depot at Ruddington, usually loaded on OLV low-sided wagons.

Another type of vehicle traffic was the dispatch of locally manufactured tractors to the Republic of Ireland, via the Fishguard to Rosslare ferry. The tractors were loaded at Coalfields on to BRV Borail wagons and were dispatched on scheduled wagonload services via Whitemoor, Bescot and Severn Tunnel Junction. This traffic ceased in 1980.

Steel traffic at Coalfields was intermittent. The main deliveries made in 1979 were several large consignments of steel sheets from Shotton (Hawarden Bridge), conveyed in a mixture of OHV, OUV, OVV, OWV, OAA and OBA open wagons, and one consignment of imported steel coil from Goole Docks, conveyed in a mixture of KNO, KCO, BEV, KDV and KGO coil wagons. Often the handling of large deliveries such as these would be spread over several days or even weeks. Of the 8 OUV wagons received on 8 February 1979, for example, two were still in the yard awaiting unloading on 1 March. Further large deliveries of steel were made from Boston Docks in May 1980 and from Lackenby in April 1981; the consignees included Acrow Tubes, Simplex and Kurvers International.

THE WAGONLOAD LEGACY

Goods traffic at Cambridge Coalfields, 1979

Incoming traffic

Commodity	Origin	Number of wagons			
		Period A	Period B	Period C	Total
Urea	Haverton Hill	35	14	42	91
Steel sheets	Hawarden Bridge	17	18	-	35
Steel coil	Goole Docks	-	-	35	35
Insulating material	Stirling	7	17	4	28
Armoured tanks	Ludgershall	-	20	-	20
Army vehicles	Donnington	-	-	20	20
Potatoes	Fearn	7	-	7	14
Fibreglass	Panteg	6	6	-	12
Paper	Salzburg, Austria	6	1	-	7
Furniture	Manzano, Italy	-	4	2	6
Plywood	Bicester	2	1	2	5
Steel plate	Hartlepool	2	1	-	3
Furniture	Udine, Italy	-	-	3	3
Tubes	Bromford Bridge	-	-	3	3
Corrugated sheet	Port Talbot	2	-	-	2
Onions	Spain	2	-	-	2
Apples	Lavaur	2	-	-	2
Army vehicle	Ludgershall	2	-	-	2
Machinery	Donnington	2	-	-	2
Coal	Hickleton	1	1	-	2
Potatoes	Montrose	1	-	1	2
Fibreglass	Wigan	-	2	-	2
Potatoes	Elgin	-	-	2	2
Lemons	?	1	-	-	1
Satsumas	?	1	-	-	1
Oranges	?	1	-	-	1
Car	Avignon	1	-	-	1
Lockers	Middlesbrough	1	-	-	1
Materials	Chilwell	1	-	-	1
Pipes	Barrow Hill	1	-	-	1
Wood packing	Donnington	1	-	-	1
Explosives	?	1	-	-	1
Cable drum	Glasgow High Street	1	-	-	1
Army trailer	Donnington	1	-	-	1
Potatoes	Dunbar	1	-	-	1
Steel plate	Port Talbot	1	-	-	1
13ft dory	Devonport	-	1	-	1
Fibreglass	Carnforth	-	1	-	1
Potatoes	Auchterarder	-	-	1	1
Potatoes	Ladybank	-	-	1	1
Furniture	S Giovanni, Italy	-	-	1	1

RAIL FREIGHT: WAGONLOAD

		Number of wagons			
Commodity	Origin	Period A	Period B	Period C	Total
Steel plate	Scunthorpe	-	-	1	1
POL products	Dinton	-	-	1	1
GPO frames	Barrow Hill	-	-	1	1
Manhole covers	Glasgow High Street	-	-	1	1
Electape	Faenza, Italy	-	-	1	1
Total		107	87	129	323

Outgoing traffic

		Number of wagons			
Commodity	Destination	Period A	Period B	Period C	Total
Army containers	Donnington	6	6	6	18
Tractors	Fishguard Harbour	6	7	-	13
Suitcases	Plymouth Friary	7	-	5	12
Herbicide	Zeebrugge	5	-	2	7
Car	Ruddington	4	2	-	6
Army vehicles	Ludgershall	-	5	-	5
Wood packing	Hawarden Bridge	-	3	-	3
Army trailers	Donnington	-	-	2	2
Straw	Whitemoor	1	-	-	1
Fork lift	Donnington	1	-	-	1
Total		30	23	15	68

Period A: 15.1.1979 to 17.3.1979
Period B: 16.4.1979 to 9.6.1979
Period C: 8.10.1979 to 7.12.1979

Trunk wagonload trains calling at Cambridge yard for traffic purposes, May 1979

Days	Arr	Dep	Train details	
MX	0219	0251	8J50	0030 Temple Mills to Whitemoor
MX	0457		8L13	0347 Whitemoor to Cambridge
SO	0635	0728	8L25	0530 Whitemoor to Great Chesterford
SX	0640	0737	8L25	0530 Whitemoor to Great Chesterford
SX		0953	8J26	0953 Cambridge to Whitemoor
SX	1549		9L23	1315 Whitemoor to Cambridge
SX	1530	1605	7J44	1448 Great Chesterford to Whitemoor (air-braked service)
SX	1716	1736	8J93	1610 Whitemoor to Temple Mills (calls at Cambridge to pick up only)
SX	2111	2150	7P06	1832 Welwyn Garden City to Whitemoor
SX	2140	2156	7J97	2043 Whitemoor to Temple Mills (calls at Cambridge to pick up only)

2.
The rise and fall of Speedlink

The launch of a fast and direct wagonload service between Bristol and Glasgow in early 1973 was BR's first move towards modernising its ailing wagonload freight network. In stark contrast to the existing wagonload operation, with its slow trains and low-capacity, short-wheelbase wagons, the new service provided a fast overnight link for traffic using BR's newly introduced long-wheelbase air-braked rolling-stock, notably the COV-AB van (later coded VAB) and the OPEN-AB open wagon (later coded OAA).

The transit time between Bristol and Glasgow was brought down to less than 12 hours, including intermediate calls at Bescot and Warrington to cater for traffic to and from those areas. The traffic on the new service included tobacco for Imperial Tobacco, chocolate for Cadbury-Schweppes, clay for English China Clay, soap powder for Procter & Gamble, newsprint for Inland Distributors, drinks for Showerings, motor vehicles for British Leyland, and aluminium for British Aluminium. BR estimated that 20% of the business was new to rail, while certain existing flows were now placed on a more secure footing thanks to the faster transit times.

BR hailed the Bristol to Glasgow service as an instant success, even though its average loadings of 24 wagons southbound and 18 northbound seem modest by 21st-century standards. BR saw the potential to introduce similar services on other routes and win more time-sensitive traffic from road competition. Going hand in hand with the new services would be the real-time control of performance through BR's new computerised Total Operations Processing System (TOPS), to be launched in stages between 1973 and 1975.

A second air-braked wagonload service, between March and Edinburgh, began in October 1973. Thereafter the network grew rapidly, with 24 services operating daily in 1976. A further boost came in that year when the Government allowed BR to invest £12 million in new air-braked rolling-stock: 300 VDA vans, 500 OBA open wagons and 200 BDA steel carriers. The VDAs and OBAs were modelled on earlier air-braked types and supplemented the 1,250 air-braked railway-owned wagons already in service, enabling BR to continue attracting customers who were unwilling to provide their own stock.

However, Speedlink also catered for privately owned vehicles that were either built with air brakes or converted for air-braked operation. Indeed, BR policy was to insist that all specialised wagons such as covered hoppers and tanks were provided by the customer. Even some palletised loads were carried in privately leased rather than railway-owned stock. In 1976 the first examples of a large fleet of 62-foot-long bogie ferry vans made their appearance on British metals, registered in Germany by Vereinigte Tanklager und Transportmittel (VTG). They were designed for cross-Channel traffic but sometimes used on domestic British flows.

In September 1977 BR Chairman Peter Parker (later Sir Peter Parker) unveiled the brand name Speedlink for BR's new wagonload network as he dispatched the Railfreight Conference train on a country-wide tour from London Marylebone. His

THE WAGONLOAD LEGACY

Above LNER-design open wagon No E295670, conveying one cable drum from Walsall Tasker Street goods depot, awaits unloading at Coalfields on 7 November 1978.

Right By the early 1960s BR had modified its standard 12-ton van design to include 9-foot sliding doors, suitable for loading palletised goods by fork-lift truck. VWV No B783035, built at Wolverton in 1961, awaits discharge at Coalfields on 13 March 1981. The straw is a tell-tale sign that on this occasion the van is carrying Scottish seed potatoes.

from the general distribution market opened the door to others. The Potter Group established a highly successful rail freight terminal on the former British Sugar factory site at Ely, which was still busy with intermodal and conventional wagon traffic in early 2006.

RAIL FREIGHT: WAGONLOAD

Tractors for shipment to Rosslare are loaded on to BRV Borail wagons at Coalfields on 11 October 1978.

Coalfields also handled a variety of packaged goods, generally conveyed in traditional VVV and VWV covered vans. The largest single flow of packaged goods was pelletised urea from Haverton Hill, bound for the Ciba-Geigy works at Duxford. This flow began to use air-braked VAB and VDA vans in February 1980 but came to an end shortly afterwards as Ciba-Geigy switched to receiving urea in bulk.

Another major flow in the 1970s was packaged insulation material from Cape Insulation at Stirling. This traffic was delivered by road from Coalfields to several different customers in the Cambridge area, including Eternit Building Products at Royston, French Kier at Newmarket and the District Council at Littleport. It declined from several wagons a week in early 1979 to just one wagonload in the first quarter of 1980. Coalfields had also handled occasional one-off consignments of fibreglass from St Helens, Wigan and Burnley.

A seasonal traffic conveyed in VVV vans was seed potatoes from various locations in Scotland, a traffic that kept many small Scottish goods stations alive long after they might otherwise have closed. One of the main forwarding points was Fearn on the Far North line, while others recorded at Cambridge between 1978 and 1981 were Elgin, Forfar, Brechin, Laurencekirk, Montrose, Auchterarder, Cupar, Ladybank, Dunbar and Dumfries.

Traffic to and from mainland Europe included seasonal deliveries of fruit and vegetables in Transfesa vans, furniture from Italy in railway-owned ferry vans, paper from Austria in VTG bogie ferry vans, and wine from Italy in railway-owned ferry vans. There was also an intermittent outward flow of agricultural chemicals bound for eastern Europe. These various flows were routed via the Dunkerque to Dover or Zeebrugge to Harwich train ferries as appropriate.

Coalfields yard lost its crane and became an unstaffed public delivery siding during the 1980s. Its last revenue-earning traffic was resin bound for Plean, a traffic that ceased with the demise of Speedlink in 1991. However, BR's withdrawal

An unusual military load for Coalfields was this vintage self-propelled anti-tank gun, which had been transported by rail from Uetendorf in Switzerland. The delicate task of unloading the gun from FIX wagon No 414 0 002-9 is pictured on 20 January 1981.

Lowfit wagon No B452855 is pictured at Coalfields on 11 October 1978, loaded with a military trailer for movement to Donnington.

THE RISE AND FALL OF SPEEDLINK

target was to have 50 Speedlink services running daily by the end of 1978, with an annual payload of 4 million tonnes – almost double the 1977 tonnage. He hoped that further growth would see 8 million tonnes on the air-braked network by 1982. He claimed that Speedlink not only covered its costs but contributed a worthwhile surplus to BR's balance sheet.

Ominously, as the Speedlink network grew, so it came to resemble the old-style wagonload network that it was designed to replace. Many of the attaching and detaching points were well established marshalling yards such as Healey Mills, Whitemoor and Severn Tunnel Junction. However, it was a cardinal principle of Speedlink that a wagon or group of wagons should be shunted no more than twice – first at the yard nearest to the loading point and then at the yard nearest to the discharge point. There should be no wholesale remarshalling of trains at intermediate locations.

The reduction in marshalling meant that BR could slim down its yards and dispense with hump operation altogether, opting instead for less labour-intensive flat shunting. At some locations this was just the logical continuation of a process that had already started in pre-Speedlink days, while other yards would see their first substantial cutbacks. However, a corollary to the rule outlawing intermediate marshalling was the need for direct trains between each of the main Speedlink yards, resulting in some lightly loaded services.

Although the streamlined operation of trunk trains was regarded as cost-effective, the organisation of trip workings to and from terminals was a harder nut to crack. In the early days of Speedlink, air-braked wagons were conveyed by old-style wagonload trip workings, which might then comprise a vacuum-braked 'fitted head' followed by Speedlink wagons with their air brake inoperative and a brake-van at the rear. This practice made it possible to serve a very large number of locations without providing extra resources. However, as traditional wagonload traffic dwindled, Speedlink movements were left to pick up a larger proportion of trip working costs.

The growth of Speedlink traffic from the late 1970s was achieved partly by winning new traffic, such as Guinness from Park Royal and an increased share of Metal Box traffic from South Wales, but more significantly by transferring existing traffic to the new operation. An easy

A contrast in rolling-stock on the 8L07 Cambridge to Newmarket trip working on 6 May 1981: No 37036 hauls nearly new air-braked Polybulks for Newmarket and 1950s-vintage unfitted mineral wagons for Brookfield cement works across Coldham's Common.

Top In the early 1980s air-braked wagons from mainland Europe were frequently conveyed in vacuum-braked trains on the British side of the Channel. Nos 20003 and 20066 depart from Tinsley with the T34 trip working to Sheffield Freight Terminal on 23 September 1980, conveying one Italian-registered ferry van and three Belgian sliding-roof vans as well as an assortment of British vacuum-braked steel-carrying wagons.

Middle No 08452 crosses the River Caldew on the Carlisle avoiding line with two empty VDA vans returning from Denton Holme Metal Box siding to Carlisle yard on 24 August 1981. The avoiding line was closed in 1984 following a serious derailment.

Below Three IPB Cargowaggon vans and ten OWV/OHV opens loaded with lime head east at Cargo Fleet on 25 March 1982, with No 31285 providing the traction. The through vacuum pipes on the IPB vans would have allowed the train to run as a vacuum-braked service, with no need for a brake-van.

THE RISE AND FALL OF SPEEDLINK

target was train ferry traffic to and from mainland Europe, as this was already conveyed in air-braked wagons. Previously ferry wagons had had to be equipped with air and vacuum brakes, or at least with air brakes and a vacuum through pipe, to allow their use on BR. In contrast to the European traffic, the transfer of domestic flows to Speedlink usually depended on the willingness of either the customer or BR to provide new stock.

On some routes the concentration of new flows was great enough to justify a new trunk service, such as the train from Hull and Doncaster that carried brandy bottles from Doncaster to France, tractors from Doncaster to Sheerness, and various products for Bisoflex, Smith & Nephew and BP Chemicals from Hull to a range of destinations. Meanwhile Metal Box increased its proportion of suitable traffic moved by rail from 50% to 90% once the reliability of Speedlink was proven.

The economic recession of the early 1980s hindered the growth of Speedlink, and Sir Peter Parker's targets proved difficult to achieve. Nevertheless, by 1981 the Speedlink network reached maturity with 11 trunk routes in place, linking all major population centres. Rather than provide further new routes, which would have brought added complexity and therefore reduced reliability to the operation, BR concentrated on 'thickening up' the network, with duplicate trains running on the busiest lines. In 1979 BR had intended that the number of trunk Speedlink services would peak at around 80 per day, but in fact it was approaching 100 by 1982.

The target load factor for trunk Speedlink services in 1981 was a modest 50%. In practice BR managed rather better loadings on most routes, with nearly 90% on the trans-Pennine axis between Warrington and Doncaster and an overall average of just under 65%. It was essential to keep some slack in the system to accommodate peaks and troughs in existing flows and to accommodate one-off or trial movements that might conceivably grow into worthwhile volumes. Although BR had to retract its aim of carrying 8 million tonnes on Speedlink by 1982, it was still optimistic of long-term growth and talked of an eventual target of 20

The Settle & Carlisle line was well used by slow freight trains that would have caused pathing difficulties on the busy West Coast Main Line. It also carried a daily Speedlink service between Severn Tunnel Junction and Mossend. No 25256 crosses Arten Gill Viaduct with 6S78, the 0205 departure from Severn Tunnel Junction, on 20 August 1981. The train includes six VEA vans, which had recently been converted from VWV Vanwides for use on military traffic.

No 46025 enters Durham station with 6M79, the 1605 Tyneside Central Freight Depot to Willesden Brent trunk Speedlink service, on 27 May 1982. The third, fourth and fifth wagons are carrying military equipment from the Royal Ordnance Factory at Birtley.

million tonnes – not far short of the tonnage carried on the old-style wagonload system. Profitability would be achieved by cutting operating costs, thanks to initiatives such as driver-only operation and flexible rostering.

Although in the early days BR was keen to market the 75mph maximum speed of Speedlink services, it turned out in practice that 60mph was adequate on most routes. Many of BR's own wagons were able to run at 75mph, but privately owned wagons were generally limited to 60mph, and the difference in overall performance achieved by the higher maximum speed was insignificant once factors such as waiting time in yards and pathing on the main line were taken into account.

The closure of the traditional wagonload network in 1983 for all freight except coal and scrap metal, and in 1984 for those two commodities, gave BR's less-than-trainload customers a stark choice: they must either convert to air-braked Speedlink operation or stop using rail. In some areas of the market BR had considerable success. Carryings of grain from East Anglia to various ports and maltings actually increased as the traffic was converted to Speedlink operation, with new Polybulk hopper wagons provided by Traffic Services Limited under the 'Grainflow' banner. The amount of grain carried on BR increased from 100,000 tonnes in 1981 to more than 300,000 tonnes in 1984.

However, in some cases the move to Speedlink was not worthwhile for the customer, who did not need the faster transit times or improved reliability compared with the traditional wagonload service and had no desire to pay higher costs. The seasonal traffic in seed potatoes from numerous Scottish loading points to equally numerous English destinations was an example of the type of business that fell by the wayside. So, too, was much of the domestic coal traffic that once formed the basis of wagonload trip workings in many parts of the country.

In the mid-1980s BR made renewed efforts to market its less-than-trainload service, using the slogan 'Speedlink – the freight name for reliability'. A number of Section 8 Grants – government money for the development of rail freight terminals, wagons and handling equipment – were primarily intended for Speedlink traffic,

THE RISE AND FALL OF SPEEDLINK

Top Sixteen miles of meandering freight-only track from Wymondham to Dereham and North Elmham remained in use for grain traffic until 1989. No 31109 approaches Wymondham with two Polybulk wagons from North Elmham to Burton-on-Trent on 17 April 1984. The train includes a brake-van for the trainman who operated the numerous level crossings on the branch. After the line closed to regular traffic it was revived as far as Dereham for occasional military loads.

Middle The last rail freight flow in the Alloa area was molasses to Menstrie. No 27063 comes off the short Menstrie branch at Cambus on 20 July 1984, hauling five empty molasses tanks for Greenock. In 2006 the line through Cambus was being prepared for re-opening as part of the Stirling-Alloa-Kincardine project, but there seemed little prospect of reviving the branch to Menstrie.

Below Pedigree Petfoods received imported offal by rail at Melton Mowbray station goods yard until the mid-1980s. No 45003 passes Frisby with four empty Interfrigo vans from Melton Mowbray on 30 July 1984.

RAIL FREIGHT: WAGONLOAD

No 08386 has just positioned four Polybulk grain hoppers for loading at Boston Docks on 31 July 1984. They had arrived on a Class 31-hauled trip working from Lincoln, which connected out of another trip working from Doncaster.

ranging from privately owned general distribution terminals such as the Cory depots at Law Junction and Cardiff Canton to industrial private siding connections such as Ciba-Geigy at Duxford and Roche Pharmaceutical Products at Dalry. BR's optimism for Speedlink was supported by a survey carried out by the Freight Transport Association among Speedlink users in 1983, in which most customers claimed that they would be increasing their use of rail in the coming year.

A market that BR targeted energetically in the 1980s was the distribution of consumer goods. In May 1983 it launched Speedlink Distribution – not a separate company or organisation as such, but a service aimed to compete with the road haulier for potentially massive pickings. The concept of Speedlink Distribution was a partnership, with BR providing trunk rail haulage but other suitably experienced private companies providing warehousing and road distribution facilities.

One distribution contract that had survived the transition from traditional wagonload to Speedlink was the Rowntrees confectionery traffic from York. BR carried Rowntrees products in railway-owned air-braked vans to a network of regional distribution terminals such as Paddock Wood, Chelmsford, Coxlodge and Perth. BR also managed to regain the small but significant flow of canned soup from Campbells at King's Lynn to Law Junction, previously lost to road because of the poor reliability of rail. Campbells was confident enough in Speedlink to invest in the long-term hire of a small fleet of curtain-sided wagons, prominently displaying the company's name.

Taunton Cider became one of Speedlink Distribution's prized customers when it opened a loading point on the rump of the former Minehead branch at Norton Fitzwarren, near Taunton, in 1983. The company built up a rail-based distribution network with receiving depots at Ely, Selby, Middlesbrough, Holyhead (for export to Ireland), Law Junction and Aberdeen. It later received Section 8 funding to lay a siding directly into its Taunton plant.

Other Speedlink users in the drinks industry were Guinness at Park Royal, Bulmers at Hereford, Newquay Steam Beer at Truro, Whiteways at Whimple and Showerings at Bridgwater. A useful development for the palletised drinks traffic was BR's VGA van, introduced in 1982 to supersede the earlier air-braked van types that had been modelled on the 1960s COV-AB. The VGA van was just over 42 feet long, which was remarkably long for a two-axle wagon, and it had two 20ft 8½in sliding doors on each side giving access to half the wagon length at a time.

The 1980s saw the setting up and expansion of a number of private distribution railheads, as BR gradually closed down its own general freight terminals. The Potter Group was one of the first companies to fill the gap in the market, opening its first rail terminal at Ely in 1981 and its second at Selby in 1983. Another successful private railhead was the Fogarty terminal at Blackburn, extended with Section 8 Grant assistance in 1983 to handle a range of traffics including steel, china clay, paper and timber. In Scotland, J. G. Russell and P. D. Stirling established sizeable distribution depots at Deanside and Mossend respectively. These two facilities, together with the previously established terminal at Law Junction, took over the role of BR's Glasgow High Street freight depot.

THE RISE AND FALL OF SPEEDLINK

Above BR used Tyne & Wear Metro tracks to reach the Rowntrees distribution terminal at Coxlodge, north of Newcastle. No 31178 propels one VDA van with attendant brake-van into the Rowntrees siding on 20 February 1984.

Below Speedlink gave the railway a second chance to carry canned soups from Campbells at King's Lynn. Two PVB curtain-sided vans travel north behind No 37140 in the consist of 6S96, the 1350 from Parkeston to Mossend, on 31 July 1984.

RAIL FREIGHT: WAGONLOAD

Cornish china clay traffic produced a remarkable variety of air-braked wagon types in the 1980s. No 46028 prepares to back out of St Blazey yard with 6C43, the 1520 feeder service to Severn Tunnel Junction, on 29 July 1983, conveying three ferry vans with bagged clay for Basel, one PBA covered hopper with bulk clay from Drinnick Mill to Cliffe Vale, one VDA van with bagged clay to Mossend, and five PRA wagons with bulk clay from Pontsmill to Corpach.

No 25229 heads away from Llandudno Junction with 7F10, the 1538 Llandudno Junction to Walton Old Junction Speedlink service, on 18 April 1985. The load includes IPB vans with aluminium ingots from Holyhead to Aachen, VDA vans with explosives from Blaenau Ffestiniog, and empty PCA cement tanks from Bangor to Penyffordd.

J. G. Russell opened its rail-served distribution depot at Deanside in 1983 on the site of a Canadian Air Force storage depot built during the Second World War. It handled a wide range of rail-borne freight in Speedlink days, as well as trainloads of Spillers petfood to and from Wisbech. No 47102 departs with the Spillers train on 12 July 1988, running as 6L80, the 1552 Deanside to Wisbech. Former BR shunter No 08345 waits for 6L80 to clear the terminal before resuming its duties.

Above Butterley Brick opened a private siding at its Boughton factory, on the Shirebrook to High Marnham line, in 1983, having previously dispatched bricks from the BR goods yard at Newark. No 37209 passes Boughton Junction with Mansfield 'target' 02 on 12 April 1984, comprising OCA and OBA wagons for loading with bricks.

Below The LCP distribution terminal at Pensnett handled a variety of rail freight flows in the 1980s, including coal, pig iron, non-ferrous metals, paper, mineral water and wine. No 45029 shunts the terminal while working the 6T42 trip from Brierley Hill on 20 August 1985. In the background is one of the two ex-BR Class 02 shunters owned by LCP.

RAIL FREIGHT: WAGONLOAD

Above No 37027 arrives at Corrour with the 0606 Sighthill to Fort William Speedlink service on 28 August 1981, conveying pulp from Methil Docks to Corpach in OBA wagons.

Below No 25201 approaches Sutton Bridge Junction, Shrewsbury, with the 6T71 trip working from Coton Hill to Welshpool on 21 August 1985. The load consists of five OBA wagons with logs from Fort William to Welshpool and two YLA wagons with rail for Hookagate permanent way depot. At that time rail-borne timber traffic was just starting to take off and BR had begun its programme of OTA conversions.

THE RISE AND FALL OF SPEEDLINK

While Speedlink Distribution targeted mainly consumer goods, further opportunities for growth in BR's wagonload business came from other sectors. In 1983 a new private siding was laid for Butterley Brick at Boughton Junction, deep in the Nottinghamshire coalfield, for wagonload consignments of bricks to various locations. At its height the Butterley traffic operated to Stratford, Norwich, Southampton, Bristol, Swansea, Gateshead, Falkirk and Aberdeen. In 1986 BR started carrying Plasmor building blocks from Heck to Biggleswade using Speedlink services. Additional destinations for the Plasmor traffic were Bow and, for a time, Wymondham.

Another traffic type that expanded rapidly in the 1980s was raw timber. The new paper mill at Shotton was geared to receiving timber by rail, and other destinations included Thames Board at Workington and Caberboard at Irvine. By 1987 the list of timber loading points included Elgin, Keith, Huntly, Inverurie, Fort William, Taynuilt, Crianlarich, Ardlui, Arrochar, Dumfries, Carmarthen and Exeter. BR quickly provided a dedicated fleet of OTA timber wagons by converting under-utilised OCA opens and VDA vans. This was the first dedicated rolling-stock for timber since the withdrawal of the vacuum-braked UUV vehicles – converted in the 1960s from plate wagons – that ran between Crianlarich and Corpach until 1979.

However, just as BR fought hard and won new customers for Speedlink, it also had to contend with the loss of some existing traffics. In 1984 Kelloggs abandoned its seemingly efficient rail operation from Trafford Park to Crawley and Hatfield. An even bigger blow was the decision by Rowntrees to stop using rail transport in 1987. The Rowntrees traffic had formed the backbone of a number of trunk Speedlink services and its demise sealed the fate of York Dringhouses yard. Many smaller losses went almost unnoticed; BR had constantly to acquire new business just to keep overall volumes stable.

By 1986 the Speedlink network comprised between 110 and 120 trunk services each weekday, together with nearly 700 trip workings of which some operated daily and others only as required. Unfortunately the trip workings consumed a disproportionate share of BR's traction and staffing resources. Many trips ran for the benefit of a single customer, often conveying just a handful of wagons and sometimes not running at all on a given day, yet still requiring the allocation of resources. Even if in theory it was possible for one trip working to remain busy all day servicing a sequence of locations, in practice this was rarely achievable because different customers tended to want servicing at the same times of day, typically an early morning arrival and a late afternoon departure.

The station goods yard at Gathurst survived after its closure to general freight in 1965 as a loading point for explosives from the nearby ICI works. No 25192 shunts VAA vans at Gathurst while working 6T72 from Warrington on 29 August 1985. The former ferry van next to the locomotive was in use as a barrier wagon, coded RBX.

RAIL FREIGHT: WAGONLOAD

Speedlink trunk trains, May 1986

Code	Days	Depart	From	To	Calling points
6S32	SuO	1600	Abercwmboi	Mossend	
6E89	SX	1435	Aberdeen	Immingham	Dundee, Millerhill, Tyne, Dringhouses, Doncaster
4M64	SX	1130	Bathgate	Willesden	Millerhill, Warrington Arpley
6F71	MX	0055	Bescot	Warrington WOJ	
7F86	MO	1317	Bescot	Warrington Arpley	Crewe
7E49	SX	1512	Bescot	Dringhouses	Derby, Tinsley
6V80	SX	2020	Bescot	Severn Tunnel Jn	
6E83	SX	2022	Bescot	Parkeston	Willesden
6S74	SX	2102	Bescot	Mossend	Warrington WOJ, Carlisle
6A21	SX	2120	Bescot	Willesden	
6E38	SX	2121	Bescot	Doncaster	Tinsley
6E93	SX	1620	Birkenhead	Whitemoor	Ellesmere Port, Peterborough, Whittlesea
6M78	SX	2155	Bridgend	Edge Hill	Severn Tunnel Jn, Halewood
7E13	SX	1454	Carlisle	Tyne Yard	
6F87	SX	2035	Carlisle	Warrington Arpley	
6V70	SX	1402	Cliffe Vale	Exeter	Stafford, Bescot, Gloucester, Stoke Gifford
6P73	MO	0609	Crewe	Warrington WOJ	
6M48	MX	0008	Dagenham Dock	Garston	Willesden, Halewood
4S39	SX	1935	Dagenham Dock	Millerhill	Doncaster
6V30	SX	2034	Dagenham Dock	Swansea	Severn Tunnel Jn
6V88	SX	2300	Dagenham Dock	Severn Tunnel Jn	Ripple Lane, Stoke Gifford
6S67	MX	0343	Doncaster	Mossend	Tyne, Millerhill
6S46	SX	1558	Doncaster	Mossend	Tyne, Millerhill
6M80	SX	2004	Doncaster	Bescot	
6V81	SX	2018	Doncaster	Severn Tunnel Jn	Stoke Gifford
6M84	SX	2110	Doncaster	Warrington Arpley	Knottingley, Healey Mills
6S73	SX	1059	Dover	Mossend	Willesden, Bletchley, Warrington WOJ
6E53	FSX	1138	Dover	Tyne Yard	Hoo Jn, Temple Mills, Offord, Doncaster, Dringhouses, Tyneside CFD
6E53	FO	1138	Dover	Tyne Yard	Hoo Jn, Temple Mills, Offord, Doncaster, Dringhouses
6M94	SX	1652	Dover	Bescot	Willesden
7M88	MX	0127	Dringhouses	Derby St Marys	Tinsley, Toton, Spondon
6S92	FSX	1908	Dringhouses	Craiginches	Tyne, Millerhill, Thornton Jn, Dundee
6S92	FO	1908	Dringhouses	Aberdeen Guild St	Tyne, Millerhill, Thornton Jn, Dundee
6O56	SX	1510	Dundee	Dover	Stirling, Mossend, Warrington Arpley, Willesden, Hoo Jn

THE RISE AND FALL OF SPEEDLINK

Code	Days	Depart	From	To	Calling points
6M84	SX	1340	Duxford	Tyne Yard	Cambridge, Ely, Whitemoor, Peterborough, Dringhouses
6E30	SX	1718	Eastleigh	Tees Yard	Oxford Hinksey, Bescot, Dringhouses
6E94	SX	2130	Eastleigh	Whitemoor	Woking, Temple Mills, Cambridge
6V91	SX	1701	Halewood	Severn Tunnel Jn	Ellesmere Port
6E85	SX	1940	Halewood	Dagenham Dock	Willesden, Ripple Lane
6O49	SX	1600	Haverton Hill	Eastleigh	Tees, Dringhouses, Bescot, Oxford Hinksey
6M64	SX	1852	Haverton Hill	Warrington Arpley	Tees, Healey Mills
7M95	MX	0150	Healey Mills	Warrington WOJ	
6V06	SX	1648	Healey Mills	Severn Tunnel Jn	Tinsley, Toton
6M57	SuO	2128	Hither Green	Bescot	Willesden
6E99	SX	1900	Hoo Junction	Tinsley	Cricklewood, Toton
6M63	SX	1510	Hull	Toton	
6M64	SX	1530	Immingham	Tyne Yard	
6E94	SuO	1639	Ince & Elton	Braintree	Peterborough, Whittlesea, Whitemoor, Ipswich
6E60	MO	0610	Millerhill	Doncaster	Tyne
6E87	SX	1750	Millerhill	Parkeston	Tyne, Dringhouses, Whitemoor, Ipswich
6E60	SO	0408	Mossend	Millerhill	
6E60	MSX	0408	Mossend	Doncaster	Millerhill, Tyne
6V93	SX	0755	Mossend	Severn Tunnel Jn	Carlisle, Warrington Arpley, Gloucester
6E97	SX	1445	Mossend	Ripple Lane	Millerhill, Whitemoor
6V92	SX	1550	Mossend	Severn Tunnel Jn	Carlisle, Hereford
6E61	SX	1630	Mossend	Doncaster	Millerhill, Tyne
6E86	SX	1920	Mossend	Parkeston	Carlisle, Tyne, Doncaster, Peterborough, Whitemoor, Ipswich
4M38	SX	2100	Mossend	Willesden	Carlisle, Bletchley
6M79	SX	2105	Mossend	Bescot	
6M28	SX	2233	Mossend	Warrington Arpley	Carlisle
6S96	SX	1345	Parkeston	Mossend	Ipswich, Whitemoor, Doncaster, Tyne, Carlisle, Law Jn
7M86	SX	1442	Parkeston	Warrington WOJ	Ipswich, Whitemoor, Toton
6D42	SX	1635	Parkeston	Doncaster	Ipswich, Whitemoor
6M86	SuO	1705	Parkeston	Bescot	
6M90	SX	1850	Parkeston	Tees Yard	Ipswich, Whitemoor, Doncaster, Dringhouses
6J62	SX	2026	Parkeston	Tinsley	Ipswich, Whitemoor, Worksop
6M88	FO	2036	Parkeston	Bescot	Willesden
6M88	FSX	2036	Parkeston	Longport	Willesden, Rugby, Bescot
6M72	SX	2148	St Blazey	Cliffe Vale	Tavistock Jn, Exeter, Gloucester

RAIL FREIGHT: WAGONLOAD

Code	Days	Depart	From	To	Calling points
6S63	SX	1330	Scunthorpe	Aberdeen	Doncaster, Tyne, Millerhill, Dundee
6E35	SX	1735	Severn Beach	Dringhouses	Hallen Marsh
6E94	MX	0125	Severn Tunnel Jn	Doncaster	Worcester, Toton
6O50	MX	0150	Severn Tunnel Jn	Dover	West Drayton, Hoo Jn
6M81	SO	0210	Severn Tunnel Jn	Crewe	
6M73	MSX	0210	Severn Tunnel Jn	Warrington WOJ	
6M75	SX	1255	Severn Tunnel Jn	Carlisle	Hereford
6E91	SX	1410	Severn Tunnel Jn	Dagenham Dock	Hallen Marsh, Ripple Lane
6M87	SX	1810	Severn Tunnel Jn	Carlisle	Hereford
6E82	SX	1820	Severn Tunnel Jn	Whitemoor	Gloucester, Bescot
6E64	SX	1915	Severn Tunnel Jn	Haverton Hill	Tinsley, Dringhouses, Tees
6M92	SX	2000	Severn Tunnel Jn	Willesden	Reading
6S82	SX	2030	Severn Tunnel Jn	Mossend	Warrington
6M83	SX	2235	Severn Tunnel Jn	Bescot	
6S57	SX	1453	Sheerness	Mossend	Queenborough, Hoo Jn, Willesden
6E96	SX	1145	Stranraer	Tyne Yard	Falkland Jn, Carlisle
6E84	SX	1525	Stranraer	Scunthorpe	Falkland Jn, Carlisle, Tyne, Dringhouses
6E95	SX	1845	Stranraer	Tees Yard	Falkland Jn, Carlisle, Tyne, Ferryhill
6E46	SX	2050	Swansea	Dagenham Dock	Severn Tunnel Jn
7S59	MX	0135	Tees Yard	Stranraer	Tyne, Carlisle, Falkland Jn
6E83	SX	1527	Tees Yard	Parkeston	Dringhouses, Doncaster, Whitemoor, Ipswich
6S66	SX	1750	Tees Yard	Stranraer	Tyne, Carlisle, Falkland Jn
6V66	SX	1835	Tees Yard	Stoke Gifford	Dringhouses
6M85	SX	1934	Tees Yard	Bescot	Tinsley
6H85	MSX	2155	Tees Yard	Duxford	Whitemoor, Cambridge
6L81	MX	0410	Tinsley	Hull	
6H91	SX	2047	Tinsley	Whitemoor	Worksop
7A84	SX	0626	Toton	Willesden	
6A82	SX	1842	Toton	Willesden	
6V56	SX	1932	Toton	Westbury	Reading
6O54	SX	2138	Toton	Hoo Jn	Willesden
6E88	SX	2000	Trostre	Whitemoor	Margam, Severn Tunnel Jn, Ketton, Peterborough
6S81	SX	2305	Tyne Yard	Mossend	
6R82	SX	1205	Tyneside CFD	Ripple Lane	Dringhouses, Doncaster, Temple Mills
6O44	FO	1605	Tyneside CFD	Hoo Jn	Dringhouses, Doncaster, Temple Mills
6O44	FSX	1605	Tyneside CFD	Paddock Wood	Dringhouses, Doncaster, Temple Mills, Hoo Jn
4R40	SX	0914	Wakefield	Dagenham Dock	Doncaster

THE RISE AND FALL OF SPEEDLINK

Code	Days	Depart	From	To	Calling points
6E63	SO	0223	Warrington Arpley	Tinsley	
6E63	MSX	0223	Warrington Arpley	Worksop	Tinsley
7A80	MSX	0406	Warrington Arpley	Willesden	Crewe, Bescot
6E95	SX	2038	Warrington Arpley	Parkeston	Toton, Whitemoor, Ipswich
6V86	SX	2150	Warrington Arpley	Severn Tunnel Jn	Hereford
6G69	SX	2215	Warrington Arpley	Bescot	
6S97	SX	0857	Warrington WOJ	Mossend	Carlisle
7E77	SX	1905	Warrington WOJ	Healey Mills	
6E80	SX	1959	Warrington WOJ	Mossend	Carlisle
6E81	SX	2058	Warrington WOJ	Haverton Hill	Dringhouses, Tees
6E26	SX	2155	Warrington WOJ	Doncaster	Healey Mills, Knottingley
6M56	FO	1940	Westbury	Toton	Reading
6E61	FSX	1940	Westbury	Worksop	Reading, Toton
6H85	MO	0437	Whitemoor	Duxford	Cambridge
6S71	SX	1903	Whitemoor	Mossend	Peterborough, Tyne, Millerhill
6V85	SX	1952	Whitemoor	Severn Tunnel Jn	Peterborough
6O90	SX	2010	Whitemoor	Eastleigh	Cambridge, Temple Mills, Woking
6V14	SX	2115	Whitemoor	Severn Tunnel Jn	Bescot
6M90	FSX	2225	Whitemoor	Birkenhead	Peterborough, Ince & Elton, Ellesmere Port
6M90	FO	2225	Whitemoor	Ellesmere Port	Peterborough, Ince & Elton
6V02	MX	0156	Willesden	Severn Tunnel Jn	Reading, Stoke Gifford
7F86	MSX	0910	Willesden	Warrington Arpley	Bescot, Crewe
7E02	SX	1254	Willesden	Worksop	Toton
6V45	SX	1753	Willesden	Severn Tunnel Jn	Swindon, Stoke Gifford
6E75	SX	2140	Willesden	Leeds Hunslet	Toton
4S48	FO	2157	Willesden	Millerhill	
4S48	FSX	2157	Willesden	Bathgate	Carlisle
6P85	SX	2216	Willesden	Workington	Warrington WOJ, Corkickle
6O38	SX	1658	Workington	Dover	Corkickle, Warrington Arpley, Willesden
6M72	SX	1946	Worksop	Warrington WOJ	Tinsley

At Temple Mills yard, on the eastern side of London, 10 of the 13 scheduled local trip departures fell between the hours of 06.00 and 12.00. In practice it would be rare for all the scheduled trip workings to run on any given day, because most customers would have days when they produced no traffic, but BR would still have to provide a locomotive and a crew, incurring costs without reaping the corresponding revenue. At Falkland Junction yard, Ayr, six separate Speedlink departures between 05.55 and 11.26 served a combined total of just eight locations.

The complexity of many Speedlink trip schedules was greater than BR had envisaged when it first promoted Speedlink. The Manchester area programme shown in the table overleaf would have required a minimum of five locomotives and rather more than five traincrew. Nevertheless it is far less complex than the programme for 1982 illustrated earlier in this volume. Many of the terminals listed in the 1982 programme were now closed, including Pendleton, Agecroft, Bolton, Reddish South and Stockport, and BR had managed to withdraw from Dewsnap

RAIL FREIGHT: WAGONLOAD

Manchester area Speedlink trips, 1986

Location	Arr	Dep	Location	Arr	Dep
7H14 MX			Castleton	1120	
Warrington Arpley		0600	**7F12**		
Peak Forest	0808		Castleton		1138
6T82			Warrington WOJ	1254	
Peak Forest		0925	**6H21 (SO)**		
Earles Sidings	1000	1045	Warrington WOJ		0504
Peak Forest	1115	1135	Trafford Park	0642	
Briggs Sidings	1215	1320	**6H21 (MSX)**		
Peak Forest	1435		Warrington WOJ		0504
7F17			Ardwick East	0609	0635
Peak Forest		1545	Trafford Park	0654	
Northenden	1625	1707	**6T80 (MO)**		
Warrington WOJ	1820		Trafford Park		0655
6H13			Ardwick East	0715	
Warrington WOJ		1413	**6T80**		
Skew Bridge	1510	1530	Ardwick East		0800
Newton Heath	1536		Ordsall Lane	0825	
6F14			Beswick	as required	
Newton Heath		1605	Ardwick East	1505	
Ordsall Lane	1623	1653	**6F32**		
Warrington WOJ	1838		Trafford Park		1705
7H15			Ashburys	1736	1756
Warrington WOJ		0636	Warrington Arpley	1855	1922
Manchester Victoria	0720		Warrington WOJ	1927	
6T85/7T85			**6P82/6F82**		
Manchester Victoria		0742	Warrington WOJ		0815
Ordsall Lane	0742		Westhoughton	0924	0954
Manchester Victoria		0830	Horwich	1111	1205
Middleton Junction	0850	1000	Chorley	1234	1356
Castleton	1020	1040	Warrington WOJ	1525	
Heywood	1050	1110			

yard and concentrate most of the wagon sorting on Warrington Arpley and Walton Old Junction yards.

If the replacement of traditional wagonload by Speedlink was meant to spell the end for wholesale marshalling, perhaps it was surprising that some of BR's marshalling yards survived as long as they did. Many yards had already declined over a long period of time, such as Carlisle Kingmoor, where the down yard closed in 1973 – barely a decade after its opening – and hump shunting in the up yard ceased in 1981. A slimmed-down flat-shunted remnant of Kingmoor survived into the 21st century.

But one significant and total closure was that of the Severn Tunnel Junction yard complex in October 1987. Traffic levels at Severn Tunnel Junction were relatively high; it was not only the gateway to South Wales but also the gathering point for wagonload traffic to and from Bristol and

Above After the closure of the Halliwell goods branch in 1981, the sidings next to Bolton station saw increased use as a public freight terminal, handling mainly steel for local distribution. No 31149 shunts wagons for 6T85, the 1555 Bolton to Ashburys trip working, on 23 May 1984. The fine LMS goods warehouse was soon to be demolished and the site sold off for redevelopment.

Middle In a setting that had obviously seen busier times, No 33012 prepares to depart from Hoo Junction yard with 6M91, the 0920 from Sheerness to Willesden, on 6 July 1987. The traffic includes an empty scrap metal carrier from Sheerness to Beeston and vans with government stores from Ridham Dock. The gantries once supported catenary enabling Class 71 locomotives to operate in overhead mode.

Bottom In 1987 yoghurt was still dispatched by rail from the Bartholomews private siding at Portfield, near Chichester. No 33042 departs from Portfield with one VBA van forming the 6Z00 trip working to Fratton on 18 August. The van will continue its journey to Scotland on 6T56 from Fratton to Eastleigh and 6E30 from Eastleigh to Haverton Hill (as far as Bescot).

RAIL FREIGHT: WAGONLOAD

BR provided a Speedlink service to several Ministry of Defence depots on Salisbury Plain. No 47236 shunts the exchange sidings at Dinton before forming 6L10, the 1223 departure to Salisbury, on 21 August 1987. The TIA tank wagon at the end of the train is on its way to Quidhampton; the sequence of scheduled calling points for this service was Eastleigh-Dean Hill-Dinton-Salisbury-Quidhampton-Salisbury-Westbury-Gloucester.

Carlisle Kingmoor was a classic 'white elephant' of the 1960s, but it survived in much reduced form as a Speedlink node and was still open for EWS Enterprise traffic in 2006. No 85021 pulls away from Kingmoor on 15 July 1988 with 6V92, the 1610 Mossend to Gloucester trunk Speedlink train, conveying a typical mixture of wagons including a PBA china clay carrier at the front and 20 VEA vans at the rear.

the West Country. Yet BR found that it was able to make huge cost savings by closing Severn Tunnel Junction and accommodating its functions elsewhere. Speedlink traffic to and from South Wales could be diverted to East Usk Junction and Cardiff Tidal yards, both locations having spare capacity alongside their main use as staging points for bulk traffic such as coal and steel. Other work previously carried out at Severn Tunnel Junction was transferred to Gloucester and Stoke Gifford, again using existing but under-utilised facilities.

The division of BR into business sectors began to have a major impact on freight operations in the mid-1980s. The distinction between bulk and non-bulk freight became very clear, with the Coal, Construction, Metals and Petroleum sub-sectors taking most bulk trainload flows while Railfreight Distribution (RfD) looked after non-bulk operations including Speedlink, automotive and chemical traffics. The bulk freight sub-sectors found that it was more cost-effective to run their own networks for less-than-trainload traffic than to continue buying into Speedlink.

The first major separation from Speedlink was domestic coal. Railfreight Coal established a dedicated network for wagonload coal traffic in three stages between November 1986 and March 1987. This network provided a service to approximately 50 coal concentration depots, using a combination of trunk trains and local trip

THE RISE AND FALL OF SPEEDLINK

Speedlink customers in the Avonmouth area included Commonwealth Smelting, the Port of Bristol Authority and Severnside Storage. On 27 July 1987 No 47245 shunts vans at Hallen Marsh Junction, Avonmouth, before working 6B17, the 1510 departure to Severn Tunnel Junction.

Although this Speedlink working looks healthily loaded, a lot of expensive shunting and trip working will be necessary for the various traffic flows to complete their journey. No 47098 passes Cogload Junction with 6B39, the 0924 St Blazey to Severn Tunnel Junction service, on 28 July 1987. The load includes an empty PLA car-carrying wagon set returning from Exeter to Halewood, VGA vans with cider from Taunton to Law Junction, OBA wagons with bricks from Plymouth to Grangemouth, PCA cement wagons returning empty from Exeter Central to Westbury and a PBA china clay wagon from Drinnick Mill to Mossend.

workings geared specifically to coal requirements. Wherever possible Railfreight Coal avoided using RfD yards, preferring to set up its own distribution centres at strategic locations. For South East England, for example, an interchange point was set up at Didcot, with trunk trains to and from South Wales and the Midlands and trip workings to individual coal depots.

In 1989 Railfreight Metals set up its own network of services for less-than-trainload flows of scrap metal and finished steel. The Metals network was based on yards at Mossend, Tees, Scunthorpe, Tinsley, Washwood Heath, Margam and Cardiff. Some former Speedlink traffic was also re-organised into block trains, such as those from Lackenby to Blackburn and from Boston to Round Oak. Only a few Metals flows, such as scrap metal from Halewood and finished steel to Holton Heath, continued to share Railfreight Distribution resources.

The opportunities for Railfreight Construction and Petroleum to withdraw from Speedlink were more limited because they produced little less-than-trainload traffic. The main type of Construction traffic conveyed by Speedlink was cement; many smaller cement flows were lost altogether from the railway in the late 1980s because of changes in the cement industry, including a rise in imports. For Railfreight Petroleum, the only significant less-than-trainload

RAIL FREIGHT: WAGONLOAD

Gloucester yard took on increased work after the closure of Severn Tunnel Junction in October 1987. No 47310 arrives at Gloucester with 6M29, the 1425 Taunton to Bescot trunk Speedlink service, on 15 February 1988. The load includes vanloads of cider from Taunton as well as five HSA wagons with scrap metal and four empty PCA cement tanks. The rake of VEA vans on the right had arrived on the 6B25 trip working from Glascoed and the single YAA wagon to the left of the VEAs had arrived on a special trip working from Worcester.

Although BR chose Willesden as the main Speedlink marshalling point for the London area, the heavily rationalised yard at Temple Mills continued to handle trip workings to and from various locations on the east side of London. On 7 July 1988 No 47157 awaits departure from Temple Mills with 7M82, one of the two daily feeder services to Willesden. It had previously arrived from Bow with the HEA hopper wagons and TTA carbon dioxide tanks visible on the right.

In 1988 the port of Stranraer generated healthy Speedlink volumes, with two scheduled trains each day and additional services as required. On 12 July No 37066 stands at Falkland Junction sidings with 6S59, the 0135 departure from Tees Yard, which normally terminated at Falkland Junction but had been extended to Stranraer on this occasion. The load comprises one BDW wagon with steel from Lackenby, one PJA set carrying cars from Longbridge, two PQA sets with cars from Cowley and Immingham, and three BDA wagons with steel from Scunthorpe, all for export to Ireland.

Scotch whisky was exported in ferry vans until the opening of the Channel Tunnel, when some flows were transferred to intermodal trains. No 26037 shunts IPB vans at the Kilmarnock distillery of Johnnie Walker on 12 July 1988, before forming the 6R05 trip working to Falkland yard.

business was gas oil to railway fuelling points. In some parts of the country, Railfreight Petroleum was able to withdraw from Speedlink either by combining long-distance flows of gas oil with commercial traffic, such as from Fawley to depots in South West England, or by serving a cluster of depots on one dedicated service, such as from Thames Haven to the London area. For the servicing of remote depots that required only occasional deliveries, such as Holyhead and Norwich, there was no realistic alternative to Speedlink.

The Speedlink network continued to provide a flexible service for wagonload traffic between Britain and mainland Europe. Such traffic was sometimes the only residual business at BR station goods yards, which, if they remained open at all, became Speedlink locations by default after 1984. The same applied to some customers' private sidings, such as BICC Prescot and Harworth Glass Bulbs, which latterly handled only European traffic. The link with the mainland was provided by the Harwich to Zeebrugge and Dover to Dunkerque train ferries. However, in an effort to cut costs and improve operating efficiencies, BR withdrew the Harwich to Zeebrugge service in January 1987 and re-routed its traffic via Dover. In the following year BR introduced its new high-capacity ferry, the *Nord Pas-de-Calais*, on the Dover to Dunkerque route. BR wished to retain and where possible increase its European business in the run-up to the opening of the Channel Tunnel.

Following the amalgamation of Railfreight Distribution and Freightliner in 1988, Speedlink's performance was placed under closer scrutiny, and it was decided to try and reduce Speedlink's costs by withdrawing lightly used services and reducing the number of marshalling points. The main changes were the abandonment of Speedlink services in the Westbury area, in West London and around Dumfries, together with withdrawal from Millerhill and Tyne yards. Economies were also achieved by combining two or more trip workings into a single service, and by reducing the duplication of services on trunk routes such as the West Coast Main Line. These alterations took effect between November 1989 and January 1990, and the resulting network was known as 'Network 90'.

RAIL FREIGHT: WAGONLOAD

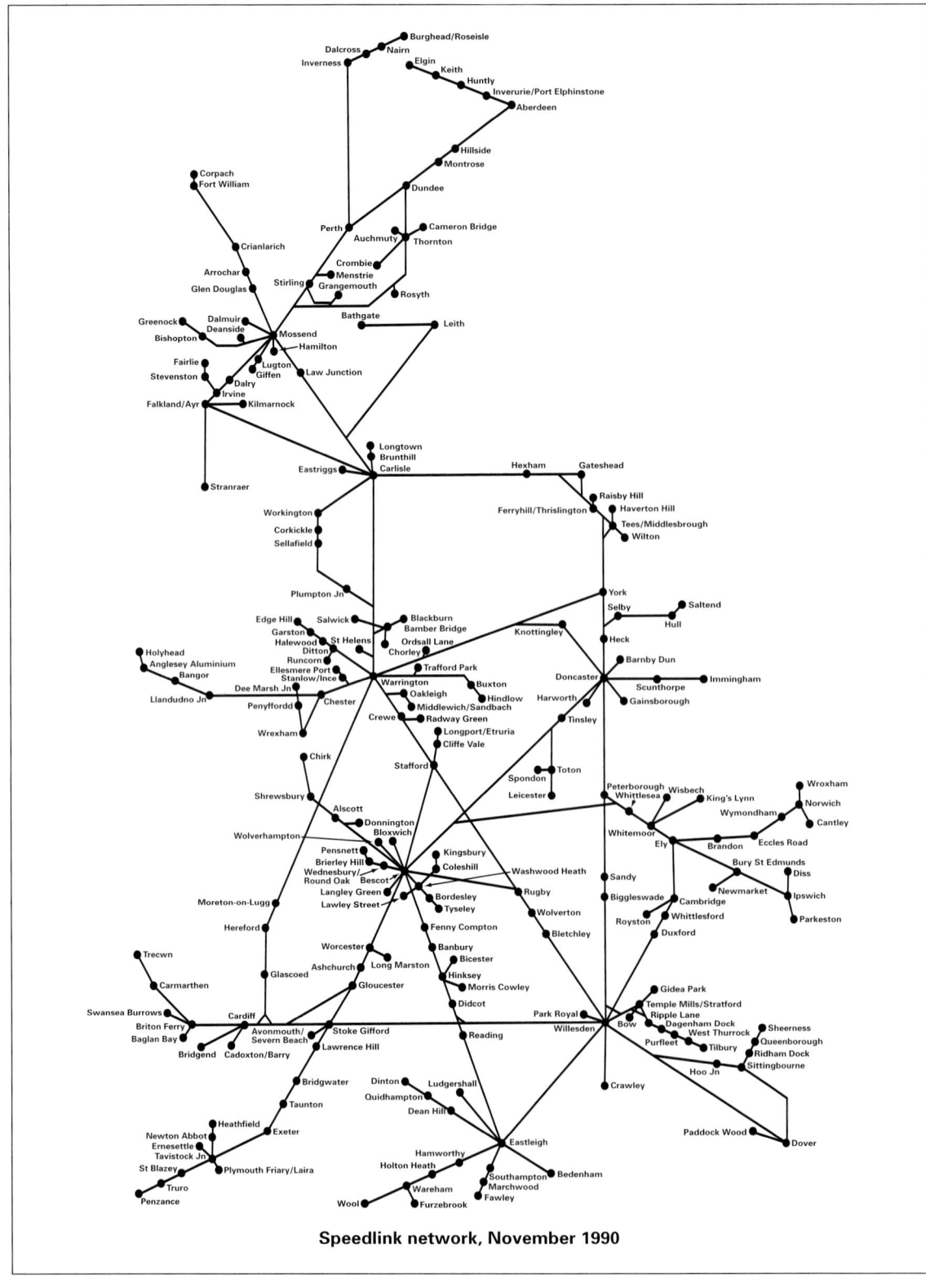

Speedlink network, November 1990

THE RISE AND FALL OF SPEEDLINK

Speedlink flows, 1990-91

Commodity	From	To
	Domestic	
Beer	Park Royal	Deanside
	Park Royal	Selby
	Park Royal	Salford
	Park Royal	Swansea
	Park Royal	Exeter
	Truro	Law Junction
	Truro	Hereford
	Truro	Taunton
Cider	Hereford	Stranraer
	Hereford	Deanside
	Hereford	Cargo Fleet
	Taunton	Stranraer
	Taunton	Law Junction
	Taunton	Cargo Fleet
	Taunton	Holyhead
Whisky	Keith	Dalmuir
Starch	Trafford Park	Aberdeen
	Trafford Park	Thornton
	Trafford Park	Sittingbourne
Molasses	Kings Lynn	Menstrie
	Peterborough	Menstrie
	Greenock	Menstrie
Sugar beet	Fletton	Gartcosh
	Fletton	Aberdeen
Preserves	Kings Lynn	Stranraer
	Kings Lynn	Law Junction
Petfood	Wisbech	Deanside
	Deanside	Wisbech
Wheat	Eccles Road	Cambus
	Newmarket	Cambus
	Newmarket	Hillside
	Kings Lynn	Deanside
Barley	Kings Lynn	Hillside
	Wroxham	Hillside
	Royston	Hillside
	Eccles Road	Hillside
	Newmarket	Burghead
	Kings Lynn	Burghead
	Eccles Road	Burghead
	Wroxham	Burghead
	Diss	Burghead
	Newmarket	Roseisle

Commodity	From	To
	Eccles Road	Roseisle
	Wroxham	Roseisle
	Diss	Roseisle
	Kings Lynn	Muir of Ord
Clay	Quidhampton	Port Elphinstone
	Burngullow	Aberdeen
	Goonbarrow	Markinch
	Quidhampton	Corpach
	Burngullow	Corpach
	Quidhampton	Mossend
	Newton Abbot	Mossend
	Marsh Mills	Mossend
	Goonbarrow	Mossend
	Burngullow	Mossend
	Parkandillack	Mossend
	Newton Abbot	Warrington
	Heathfield	Cliffe Vale
	Pontsmill	Cliffe Vale
	Furzebrook	Cliffe Vale
	Aberdeen	Sittingbourne
	Quidhampton	Sittingbourne
	Par Harbour	Duxford
Paper	Corpach	Cowley
Lime	Dowlow	Barnby Dun
	Dowlow	Mossend
	Thrislington	Inverurie
	Ferryhill	Montrose
Timber	Inverness	Shotton
	Nairn	Shotton
	Elgin	Shotton
	Keith	Shotton
	Huntly	Shotton
	Inverurie	Shotton
	Montrose	Shotton
	Fort William	Shotton
	Crianlarich	Shotton
	Carmarthen	Shotton
	Swansea	Shotton
	Cardiff	Shotton
	Exeter	Shotton
	Norwich	Chirk
	Ipswich	Chirk
	Brandon	Chirk
	Hoo Junction	Chirk

RAIL FREIGHT: WAGONLOAD

Commodity	From	To	Commodity	From	To
	Keith	Stirling		Cameron Bridge	Willesden
	Huntly	Stirling		Mossend	Newton-le-Willows
	Inverurie	Stirling		Mossend	Bow
	Keith	Irvine		Haverton Hill	Bow
Acetic acid	Saltend	Seal Sands		Haverton Hill	Willesden
	Saltend	Spondon	Salt	Runcorn	Dalry
	Saltend	Baglan Bay		Middlewich	Dalry
Nitric acid	Ince & Elton	Salwick	Fertiliser	Ince & Elton	Aberdeen
Alcohols	Baglan Bay	Purfleet		Ince & Elton	Thornton
	Baglan Bay	Saltend		Ince & Elton	Ely
Chlorine	Runcorn	Wilton		Immingham	Aberdeen
	Sandbach	Fawley		Immingham	Brunthill
Caustic soda	Runcorn	Stevenston		Immingham	Alscott
	Runcorn	Purfleet		Immingham	Carmarthen
	Immingham	Corkickle		Immingham	Holton Heath
	Immingham	Dalry		Drinnick Mill	Mossend
	Immingham	Wigton		Drinnick Mill	Selby
	Seal Sands	Dalry	Oil for BR fuelling point	Grangemouth	Aberdeen
	Sandbach	Dalry		Grangemouth	Thornton
	Sandbach	Grangemouth		Lindsey	Heaton
	Purfleet	Fawley		Lindsey	Thornaby
Soda ash	Oakleigh	Barnby Dun		Lindsey	Shirebrook
Gases	Parkeston	Barry		Stanlow	Longsight
Resin	Duxford	Dalcross		Stanlow	Holyhead
	Duxford	Irvine		Stanlow	Chester
	Duxford	Stranraer		Stanlow	Buxton
	Duxford	Hexham		Stanlow	Leicester
	Duxford	Middlesbrough		Stanlow	Peterborough
	Cambridge	Plean		Stanlow	March
Methanol	Purfleet	Duxford		Stanlow	Cambridge
	Haverton Hill	Eastleigh		Stanlow	Norwich
	Haverton Hill	Langley Green		Thames Haven	Ipswich
Corrosive chemicals	Spondon	Saltend		Thames Haven	Chart Leacon
	Saltend	Mostyn		Thames Haven	Dover
Sodium tripolyphosphate	Corkickle	West Thurrock	Lubricating oil	Ellesmere Port	Laira
Solvents	Saltend	Plumpton Jn	Oil	Stanlow	Llandudno Jn
	Saltend	Dalry		Parkeston	Aberdeen
	Saltend	Spondon		Parkeston	Longport
Sulphuric acid	St Helens	Dalry		Fawley	Cambridge
Urea	Kings Lynn	Duxford	Aviation fuel	Long Marston	Warrington
Oxygen	Ditton	Sheerness	Propane	Seal Sands	Elgin
Carbon dioxide	Cameron Bridge	Newton-le-Willows		Grangemouth	Aberdeen
			Motor vehicles	Garston	Exeter
				Longbridge	Stranraer

THE RISE AND FALL OF SPEEDLINK

Commodity	From	To	Commodity	From	To
	Cowley	Stranraer	Industrial		
	Sheerness	Leith	sand	Kings Lynn	Law Junction
Government	Crombie	Bedenham	Coal	Littleton	Bicester
stores	Crombie	Trecwn	Steel	Lackenby	Dundee
	Rosyth	Hessay	sections	Lackenby	Holton Heath
	Rosyth	Southampton	Tubes	Corby	Dundee
	Stirling	Ludgershall	Scrap metal	Workington	Aldwarke
	Giffen	Ernesettle			
	Powfoot	Lawley Street			
	Longtown	Trecwn			
	Longtown	Ridham Dock			
	Longtown	Marchwood			
	Longtown	Wool			
	Long Marston	Stirling			
	Long Marston	Warrington			
	Ashchurch	Marchwood			
	Swindon	Donnington			
	Bicester	Donnington			
	Bicester	Wolverhampton			
	Bicester	Ludgershall			
	Bicester	Ashford			
	Bicester	Ripple Lane			
	Bicester	Millbrook			
	Dean Hill	Glen Douglas			
	Bedenham	Glen Douglas			
	Marchwood	Long Marston			
	Plymouth	Rosyth			
	Ernesettle	Crombie			
Electrical	Bodmin	Leith			
goods	Bodmin	Warrington			
	Bodmin	Gidea Park			
	Bodmin	Stratford			
Containers	Elgin	Holyhead			
	Bristol	Coatbridge			
	Coatbridge	Bristol			
Cement	Eastgate	Grangemouth			
	Eastgate	Northenden			
	Eastgate	Handsworth			
	Eastgate	Harbury			
	Oxwellmains	Irvine			
	Penyffordd	Bangor			
Bricks	Plymouth	Grangemouth			
Blocks	Heck	Wymondham			
	Heck	Biggleswade			
	Heck	Bow			

Import via train ferry

Commodity	To
Fruit	Deanside
	Middlesbrough
	Ely
	Ripple Lane
	Stratford
Preserves	Ely
Wine	Bamber Bridge
	Wavertree
	Wakefield
	Pensnett
	Eastleigh
Mineral water	Salford
	Pensnett
	Lawley Street
	Ely
	Stratford
	Ashford
	Crawley
Malt	Keith
	Eccles Road
Chipboard	Blackburn
	Sandy
	Gidea Park
	Crawley
Wood products	Blackburn
	Eastleigh
Glass	Lawley Street
Timber	Ditton
Paper	Salford
	Trafford Park
	Cowley
	Gidea Park
Silica	Trafford Park
	Bamber Bridge
Slag	Trafford Park

RAIL FREIGHT: WAGONLOAD

Commodity	To
Hardstone	Trafford Park
Rock salt	Ely
Clay	Ely
Alcohols	Middlesbrough
Gases	Middlesbrough
	Kings Lynn
Resin	Ellesmere Port
	Cowley
Metallic compounds	Grangemouth
	Trafford Park
Plastics	Ellesmere Port
Corrosive chemicals	Selby
	Shotton
Octel	Ellesmere Port
Dangerous chemicals	Shotton
Non-dangerous chemicals	Middlesbrough
	Bamber Bridge
	Ashford
Phosphorus	Langley Green
Refrigerants	Trafford Park
Metal products	Pensnett
Cables	Warrington
	Wolverhampton
	Wednesbury
Electrical goods	Paddock Wood
Machinery	Whittlesea
Textiles	Wakefield
Clothing	Deanside
Leather goods	Lawley Street
Bricks	Middlesbrough
Steel tubes	Mossend
Steel	Mossend
	Warrington
	Trafford Park
	Sheffield
	Wednesbury
	Round Oak
	Brierley Hill
	Ripple Lane
Aluminium	Selby
Non-ferrous metals	Bloxwich

Export via train ferry

Commodity	From
Whisky	Perth
	Deanside

Commodity	From
	Kilmarnock
	Barleith
Starch	Trafford Park
Potatoes	Montrose
Petfood	Wisbech
Other food	Wakefield
Clay	Drinnick Mill
	Par Harbour
	Marsh Mills
	Exeter
	Furzebrook
Paper	Aberdeen
	Shotton
Gases	Haverton Hill
	Grimsby
Hydrocarbons	Amlwch
Metallic compounds	Wilton
Alcohols	Middlesbrough
Corrosive chemicals	Avonmouth
Octel	Ellesmere Port
Plastics	Trafford Park
	Barry
Synthetic rubber	Grangemouth
Solvents	Spondon
Pharmaceuticals	Dalry
Other chemicals	Wilton
	Warrington
	Trafford Park
	Selby
	Ely
	Gidea Park
Bauxite	Thornton
Aluminium	Deanside
	Lynemouth
	Holyhead
	Cardiff Canton
Non-ferrous metals	Wolverhampton
	Avonmouth
	Ripple Lane
Steel products	Law Junction
Steel ingots	Mossend
Steel	Skinningrove
	Immingham
	Scunthorpe
	Aldwarke
	Thrybergh

THE RISE AND FALL OF SPEEDLINK

Commodity	From	Commodity	From
	Sheffield	Steel tubes	Round Oak
	Etruria	Bricks	Longport
	Port Talbot	Textiles	Wakefield
	Cardiff Tremorfa	Groupage traffic	Trafford Park
	Cardiff Rod Mill	Nuclear flasks	Sellafield
	Llanwern	Government stores	Longtown
	Sheerness		

While Speedlink faced rationalisation, BR was still pursuing new wagonload business. The Caledonian Paper mill at Irvine opened to rail traffic in 1989 and handled wagonload deliveries of timber as well as trainloads of china clay. Cerestar started using the Trafford Park Estates railway to dispatch wagonloads of starch via Speedlink to Sittingbourne and Aberdeen. And Kronospan opened a siding at its Chirk manufacturing site to receive wagonloads of timber from East Anglian railheads such as Ipswich and Brandon. Short-term traffic opportunities included the movement of windfall timber from Ashford, Hoo Junction, Crawley and Chichester, following the devastating storms of October 1987.

However, the amalgamation of Railfreight Distribution and Freightliner did not lead to 'containers by the wagonload' on any significant scale: the only example of shared operation was a nightly service on the Marches line that carried Freightliner boxes between Bristol and Coatbridge as well as conventional wagonloads of cider from Hereford to depots in northern England and Scotland.

The dust had hardly settled on Network 90 when a much more searching review of Speedlink's financial performance was carried out. The Speedlink network was found to be losing £30 million a year on a turnover of only £45 million, and Network 90 had done little more than tinker with the periphery of a very major problem. The Speedlink Review of 1990, then, examined every existing Speedlink flow in detail and analysed its costs in terms of tripping, marshalling and trunk haulage. The outcome of the Review was damning: every single Speedlink flow was a loss-maker. In order to ensure that all the costs were covered, a Speedlink customer would need to generate at least ten wagonloads a day over a distance of at least 500 miles, which simply could not be marketed on an island the size of Britain.

The Trafford Park Estates railway in Manchester re-opened in late 1988, initially for scrap metal from Norton Metals and later for starch from Cerestar. The railway acquired two ex-BR Class 08 shunters to move wagons between the loading terminals and Trafford Park exchange sidings. No 08423 awaits authority to leave the Cerestar works on 4 September 1989 with one PBA wagon destined for Thornton Junction, two PCA wagons for Sittingbourne, and one PBA wagon for Aberdeen.

RAIL FREIGHT: WAGONLOAD

An intricate Speedlink operation in summer 1990 was an out-and-back working from Warrington, serving Blackburn (Fogartys distribution depot), Bamber Bridge (W. H. Bowker distribution depot), Chorley (Royal Ordnance Factory) and Salwick (British Nuclear Fuels). The same locomotive would also usually work early-morning and late-evening trips between Warrington and the Otis distribution depot at Ordsall Lane. On 6 April No 47142 has just arrived at Blackburn with 6N73, the 0847 departure from Warrington. The train has been divided into four portions: one ZBA engineers' wagon for Blackburn station, five VEA vans for Chorley, one IUA hooded wagon for Bamber Bridge, and one IPB van for Fogartys at Blackburn. On the right is No 37058, which has arrived on the 6M58 steel train from Lackenby.

The BR freight terminal at Warrington Dallam remained in use until the end of Speedlink for flows of steel from South Wales and imported goods via the Dunkerque to Dover train ferry. No 08809 shunts the terminal on 10 April 1990 before taking the empty wagons on the right back to Arpley yard.

Above On the truncated line that once formed a through route from Wellington to Stafford, No 47238 draws to a halt at Donnington exchange sidings on 9 July 1990, having brought a single VGA van from Shrewsbury Coton Hill yard. On this occasion there was no outward traffic from Donnington and the locomotive returned light to Shrewsbury. In 2005 hopes were raised that the Donnington branch might re-open, both for military traffic and for general freight.

Below Hereford station goods yard remained active until the final years of Speedlink with steel, timber and cider traffic. The resident pilot locomotive, No 09015, pulls four VDA, VGA and VBA vans out of the yard on 9 July 1990, ready to be attached to 6S74, the 1954 departure to Coatbridge.

Above No 37015 passes Ferryside with 6B54, the 0515 Gloucester to Trecwn Speedlink feeder service, on 11 July 1990. The traffic comprises VDA and VEA vans with government stores for Trecwn and IPA vans with fertiliser from Immingham to Carmarthen.

Middle No 47245 departs from Corkickle with 6A40, the 1640 Workington to Willesden Speedlink service, on 24 July 1990. The train comprises six PCA tanks with sodium tripolyphosphate from Corkickle to West Thurrock, YAA and YLA wagons with rails from Workington, and ten TTA caustic soda tanks returning empty from Corkickle to Runcorn.

Bottom The former Midland Railway goods yard at Bow continued to receive wagonloads of coal, building blocks and carbon dioxide in 1990. The wagons were tripped from Temple Mills in the early morning and back in the afternoon. No 08709 shunts one HEA hopper with industrial coal from Gedling and several TTA carbon dioxide tanks at Bow on 2 August.

Above The rump of the former Swanage branch received regular visits from Speedlink trip working 6W51/6W56 to serve the English China Clay works at Furzebrook, in addition to block trains of liquefied petroleum gas from the adjacent Wytch Farm loading terminal. No 47144 shunts 6W51, the 0803 departure from Eastleigh, at Furzebrook on 14 August 1990. It has just collected the two PBA clay wagons from the ECC siding and will attach them to the two BDA steel carriers and one IPA fertiliser van before departing as 6W56 to Eastleigh. The BDAs and IPA will be detached en route at Holton Heath.

Below The short Auchmuty branch in Fife required the use of a brake-van because it had no run-round facility and trains had to be propelled on the return journey. No 08761 brings up the rear of the 9G14 trip working arriving at Thornton on 28 August 1990, conveying one empty PBA and two empty PAA clay hoppers.

The comparative remoteness of Aberdeen and therefore its greater potential for long-distance traffic meant that it was a busier Speedlink location than most other cities of similar size. No 47347 passes Carnoustie on 29 August 1990 with a particularly heavily loaded 6M64, the 1232 Aberdeen to Willesden service. The main ferry van traffic from Aberdeen at that time was paper.

Grangemouth became the gathering point for Speedlink traffic to and from Larbert, Stirling, Menstrie, Cambus, Polmaise and Plean, as well as Grangemouth itself. No 26040 departs with 6N06 to Mossend on 30 August 1990, its load including empty PCA cement tanks from Grangemouth to Oxwellmains, empty OCA wagons returning from Grangemouth to Plymouth, and empty TTA molasses tanks from Menstrie to Peterborough or King's Lynn.

BR considered four options for the future of Speedlink. The first was to reduce Speedlink to a 'core network' in an attempt to achieve profitability – a further refinement on Network 90, perhaps. But previous attempts to reduce Speedlink's costs in this way had had little effect, and Speedlink's customers were too widely scattered geographically for any profitable core network to be established. The second option was to increase the marketing effort and win new traffic flows. But a survey of 30,000 companies who might have suitable traffic to offer brought a negligible response, and, even if new flows were acquired, this would lead to an increase in local trip working and marshalling that accounted for more than 70% of Speedlink's costs. The third option was to cut costs within the current network. But even if a massive saving of 40% were to be achieved, only 15% of current Speedlink flows would become profitable. The fourth option was total withdrawal from the less-than-trainload market.

The decision to close Speedlink down was taken by the British Railways Board on 6 December 1990, to take effect from 8 July 1991. RfD was at pains to point out the relatively small volume of freight involved: in its last full year of operation Speedlink carried only 2.3% of BR freight, and just 0.12% of all freight in the UK. Furthermore, over half of Speedlink's carryings would be accommodated on other services, with block trains for some domestic customers and dedicated RfD International services for train ferry traffic. Nevertheless it was sad to see the end of BR's countrywide wagonload service, only three years before the opening of the Channel Tunnel and the expected increase in freight traffic between Britain and mainland Europe.

THE RISE AND FALL OF SPEEDLINK

Above With just ten days to go before the demise of Speedlink, No 08916 shunts a PAA wagon with lime from Dowlow to Mossend and two IPA vans with fertiliser from Ince & Elton to Lugton at Warrington Walton Old Junction yard on 25 June 1991. The three wagons will travel north on 6S80 to Mossend.

Below On 5 July 1991, the very last day of Speedlink, No 90028 passes Farington with 6S97, the 0103 Gloucester to Mossend trunk service.

RAIL FREIGHT: WAGONLOAD

Train ferries

Two commercial train ferry services between Britain and mainland Europe were established before the Second World War: the Harwich to Zeebrugge route was opened by Great Eastern Train Ferries Limited in 1924 and the Dover to Dunkerque operation was launched by the Southern Railway in 1936. The latter carried not only freight wagons but also the famous 'Night Ferry' overnight passenger service from London to Paris and Brussels.

Both train ferry routes survived into the BR era, coming under the management of BR's shipping arm Sealink. Whereas the 'Night Ferry' was withdrawn in 1980, the freight traffic via Dover and Harwich was gradually integrated into the expanding Speedlink network. However, the costs of operating the ferries were high – one wagon-kilometre by train ferry was about ten times as expensive as one wagon-kilometre on the railway. Sealink therefore closed down the longer-distance Harwich to Zeebrugge operation in January 1987 and concentrated all traffic on the shorter Dover to Dunkerque route. A single ship could make three daily return trips between Dover and Dunkerque, compared with only one return trip between Harwich and Zeebrugge.

Even after train ferry resources were concentrated on the Dover to Dunkerque route, its efficiency was hampered at first by the need to use two separate ships, each having only limited capacity for rail traffic. In January 1988 Sealink replaced those ships with a single purpose-built high-capacity vessel, the *Nord Pas-de-Calais*. This was able to carry both road and rail traffic; the upper deck was for road vehicles only, while the main deck could be used for road vehicles, railway wagons or a combination of the two. The railway capacity comprised six sidings, with a total usable track length of 600 metres, which enabled up to 30 average-sized bogie wagons to be carried on each crossing. Unlike the Channel Tunnel service that would soon replace it, the train ferry was for conventional wagons only and its operator had no ambition to carry rail-borne intermodal or motor vehicle traffic.

The *Nord Pas-de-Calais* had a horsepower rating of 24,500. Its normal service speed was 21.5 knots, which was about 25% faster than most other cross-Channel ferries. This meant that it could cross the Channel in less than 2 hours and make an extra return journey each day if required. A notable design feature of the ship was that the main deck included an uncovered section at the stern end, isolated from the rest of the deck by watertight doors. This was designated for use by dangerous loads, especially toxic or flammable materials.

At both ends of its route, the *Nord Pas-de-Calais* used purpose-built berthing facilities. Those at Dover cost a total of £15 million when completed in 1987. The ingenious part of the installation was the linkspan. This consisted of three sections, the two outer able to move with the tide but with the change of angle at the joints limited to 2.5 degrees up or down. Loading could therefore take place whatever the state of the tide, and it also allowed for some up and down movement as wagons are shunted off and on to the ship. The linkspan for the old ferries did not need to have this degree of flexibility as it was located inside a locked dock, ie one separated from the sea by a lock so that the water level inside it was kept constant.

When the new tilting linkspan was first commissioned, the task of hauling wagons on and off the ship switched from Class 09 to Class 33/2 traction because the Class 09 wheelbase was believed to be too rigid for comfortable operation. However, the designated Class 33/2s became increasingly unreliable and BR reverted to using Class 08s and 09s in 1993, which turned out to be well suited to the task.

In 1993 the *Nord Pas-de-Calais* was scheduled to make three return trips each weekday, with a fourth path available for busy periods. The actual volume of rail freight amounted to roughly a million tonnes each year. The origin and destination points in mainland Europe were spread far and wide, but the countries producing the most business were France, Germany and Italy, as shown in the accompanying table. The reason why Italy produced a lower tonnage but a greater number of wagons is that one of the principal Italian traffics was electrical products or 'white goods', which are comparatively light in weight.

In mainland Europe most train ferry traffic was conveyed by normal wagonload services. Although there was an extensive marshalling yard

Above An overall view of Dover Town yard on 16 July 1987, as 6M94, the 1652 Speedlink service to Bescot, pulls out on to the main line. Most of the wagons visible in the yard are on their way to or from mainland Europe; however, the Land Rovers in the foreground will be unloaded at Dover and driven on to the ferry.

Below Shunting the old linkspan sidings at Dover Hawkesbury Street Junction on the same day are Nos 09018 and 09021. By this time most ferry traffic was loaded in bogie wagons, but the Class 09-hauled rake on the right includes two Transfesa two-axle ITX vans. These sidings were abandoned when the new linkspan on the seaward side of Dover Western Docks station came into use.

RAIL FREIGHT: WAGONLOAD

Left Nos 08698 and 09016 share the task of unloading the *Nord Pas-de-Calais* at Dover on 17 February 1994. Loading and unloading was always carried out on both tracks simultaneously in order to maintain the correct balance of cargo on the vessel's railway deck.

Below Shunting at Dunkerque train ferry terminal was carried out by permanently coupled 'master and slave' units of Class 64700/64800. This view, also dated 17 February 1994, shows Nos 64818 and 64718 nearest the camera, with Nos 64702 and 64802 on the adjacent track.

Train ferry business, 1993		
Origin/destination	Freight (tonnes)	No of wagons
France	321,825	6,619
Germany	216,588	4,046
Italy	167,122	4,231
Others	202,432	5,030
Total	907,967	19,926

at Dunkerque Grande Synthe, most of the sorting was carried out instead at one of two large SNCF yards in the Lille area – Lille La Délivrance and Somain. Both yards were served by regular feeder services to and from Dunkerque. Trunk services operated between either Lille La Délivrance or Somain and a wide range of European destinations. Somain handled traffic bound for northern France, the Benelux countries and Great Britain, while Lille La Délivrance dispatched trains to southern France. The only direct long-distance ferry wagon service from Dunkerque in 1993 was one carrying china clay to northern Italy.

The introduction of the *Nord Pas-de-Calais* kept rail freight moving between Britain and mainland Europe in the period running up to the opening of the Channel Tunnel. But any hopes of increasing traffic volumes in that period were dashed. The progressive decline in wagonload freight networks on both sides of the Channel led to the loss of a number of small-scale flows, and the trend towards even larger wagons – notably the 27-metre-long IZA twin vans – meant that the wagon space on the ferry was less efficiently used and the total payload per crossing was reduced.

Once the Tunnel was open, the Dover to Dunkerque train ferry was effectively dead. The French operator SNCF tried to keep the ferry operating for hazardous cargoes that were barred from the Tunnel. However, the volume of such traffic was too low for continued operation to be viable, even if the spare capacity on each sailing were to be taken up by road vehicles. The costs of maintaining and operating the linkspans alone could not be justified by the available tonnages. The decision was therefore made to abandon the train ferry service and the *Nord Pas-de-Calais* carried its last consignment of rail freight on 22 December 1995. The ship was then redeployed as a SeaFrance vehicle ferry between Dover and Calais and renamed *SeaFrance Nord Pas-de-Calais*.

Proposals to re-instate a cross-Channel train ferry service, from either Dover or Harwich, have been publicised from time to time in recent years. However, with the Tunnel struggling to maintain its pitiful share of the cross-Channel freight market and with road haulage becoming ever more dominant, it is difficult at the time of writing to see how a revived train ferry service could pay its way.

A Speedlink case study: Ciba-Geigy, Duxford

Under Section 8 of the 1974 Railways Act, the Government part-funded many new freight terminals, as well as the upgrading of existing terminals and the provision of rolling-stock and handling equipment. A typical example was the building of a new rail freight terminal for the Ciba-Geigy chemical plant at Duxford, the £940,000 cost of which was supported by a £470,000 grant in August 1979. The terminal became fully operational in October 1980 and for more than a decade it handled a wide variety of freight flows, mainly using the national Speedlink network.

Ciba-Geigy was formed in 1971 by the merger of Swiss-owned chemical firms CIBA and J. R. Geigy. The Duxford manufacturing site, which had been established since before the Second World War, housed the Plastics division of the company, producing a range of epoxy resins, formaldehyde-based resins and composite materials. Although the site lay less than a quarter of a mile from the main London to Cambridge line, early proposals to install a private siding came to nothing. BR saw little incentive to pay towards a connection because Ciba-Geigy was already a major user of the public goods terminals at Great Chesterford, Whittlesford and Cambridge, and a new private siding would merely divert existing traffic.

However, attitudes changed during the 1970s. Ciba-Geigy became increasingly concerned about the impact of its heavy lorry traffic in the villages of Duxford and Ickleton, especially as some of the

RAIL FREIGHT: WAGONLOAD

lorries carried highly inflammable loads. BR had closed down most of its local goods yards and had little reason to retain the Great Chesterford and Whittlesford depots other than for the Ciba-Geigy business. But without doubt it was the availability of Section 8 funding that clinched the decision to go ahead with a private siding at the Ciba-Geigy plant.

The new railway infrastructure for Duxford consisted of a single-lead trailing connection from the down main line, six sidings for loading and unloading traffic, and a weighbridge. The sidings comprised three distinct groups: two sidings parallel to the BR main line for receiving tankloads of methanol, three sidings on the south side of the main factory site for handling urea and other bulk materials, and one siding running through the middle of the site for the loading of liquid resins.

BR locomotives propelled each arriving train into the Duxford site and could shunt all sidings except for the liquid resin line. No run-round facility was necessary because trains arrived from the south and departed to the north. For internal shunting, Ciba-Geigy owned two traction units: a Unilok machine supplied from Dublin, able to pull loads up to 600 tonnes, and a Mercedes-Benz Unimog locomotive with a haulage capacity of 800 tonnes. These units had both rubber tyres and flanged wheels, giving a high degree of flexibility around the site.

When the terminal first opened, the main traffic flows using it were granulated urea and methanol, both originating at Haverton Hill on Teesside. The urea flow benefited from newly converted PAA covered hopper wagons, supplied to ICI with Section 8 assistance to accompany the Ciba-Geigy scheme. The methanol was carried in existing TTB tank wagons.

The urea and methanol flows became the staple traffic on a direct Speedlink service from Haverton Hill to Duxford, which had previously run only as far as Whitemoor. The train was scheduled to reach Duxford in the early morning, enabling Ciba-Geigy staff to begin unloading the wagons at the start of the working day.

That service still conveyed traffic for other customers and continued to make intermediate calls at Tees Yard and Whitemoor, but Ciba-Geigy typically provided more than half of its payload. Outgoing traffic and empty wagons returning to Teesside were conveyed by an early afternoon Speedlink trip working from Duxford to Whitemoor, connecting at March Down yard with trunk services to Mossend and Severn Tunnel Junction. BR later introduced a direct Speedlink service from Duxford to Tyne Yard.

During the 1980s the urea and methanol were joined by a wide variety of other flows, making good use of the national Speedlink network. By the end of the decade, the total rail-borne traffic at Duxford had grown to about 140,000 tonnes a year. Outgoing traffic included liquid resin for the manufacturing of chipboard, mainly to Hexham

Ciba-Geigy's Mercedes Unimog vehicle manoeuvres a rake of JIA/JIB urea wagons at the discharge hopper house on 26 July 1991. On the left is the company's Unilok machine, built by the German firm Hugo Aeckerle & Co.

Above Ciba-Geigy made extensive use of the Speedlink network. No 40192 passes Stockton with the 1605 Haverton Hill to Parkeston trunk Speedlink service on 18 March 1981, consisting entirely of traffic for Duxford: TTB tanks with methanol and PAA wagons with urea.

Below A mixed Speedlink and vacuum-braked feeder service for Whitemoor yard leaves Cambridge on 6 May 1981. The first half of the train comprises empty methanol tanks and empty urea wagons from Duxford to Haverton Hill; the remainder is made up of Polybulk and traditional grain hoppers bound for Barry, Birkenhead and Muir of Ord.

RAIL FREIGHT: WAGONLOAD

No 47309 departs from the Ciba-Geigy sidings at Duxford with the 1238 trip working to Whitemoor on 7 August 1990. The train consists of tank wagons with resin for Hexham and empty Polybulk hoppers returning to King's Lynn for reloading with urea.

(up to 35,000 tonnes a year), but also in smaller quantities to Stirling, Taunton and Stranraer for export to Ireland. For these flows Ciba-Geigy hired a pool of two-axle and bogie tank wagons that had originally been built for petroleum traffic. Resin was also conveyed in powdered form to Dalcross, near Inverness.

Incoming flows, apart from the urea and methanol mentioned above, included one weekly delivery of china clay from Par, together with occasional deliveries of packaging from Dundee and olive stone flour from Bridgwater or Taunton. These three flows were carried in VGA vans. Duxford also became the receiving point for tankloads of herbicide from Basel, destined for Ciba-Geigy's Agrochemicals division at nearby Whittlesford.

In 1989 Ciba-Geigy's Duxford operation was taken over by Dynochem, the UK division of Dyno Industries. That takeover brought a number of changes to the company's transport requirements. Dyno's manufacturing interests included the production of both urea and methanol, so there was no longer any need for Ciba-Geigy to buy these materials from ICI on Teesside.

The supply of urea passed to Hydro, the parent company of Dyno, which had its main manufacturing plant in the Netherlands. The urea was brought to King's Lynn in 1,000-tonne shipments and railed from King's Lynn to Duxford in bogie Polybulk wagons, which Hydro leased from Mineralhaul.

The sourcing of methanol changed to Methanor, a Dutch company with 30% Dyno ownership. Again, a combination of sea and rail transport was used. The methanol arrived at Purfleet in 4,000-tonne shipments and was moved from Purfleet to Duxford in newly built bogie tank wagons hired from Tiphook.

The existing Speedlink network accommodated

THE RISE AND FALL OF SPEEDLINK

No 37272 positions its rake of TTA tanks in the methanol discharge siding at Duxford on 26 July 1991, having arrived with the 1030 contract train from Purfleet.

the new flows of urea and methanol. The urea travelled on scheduled feeder services from King's Lynn to Whitemoor and from Whitemoor to Duxford. The methanol used an existing feeder service from Purfleet to Willesden, the overnight Eastleigh to Whitemoor service between Willesden and Cambridge, and an existing feeder service from Cambridge to Duxford.

A problem arose sometimes when the Eastleigh to Whitemoor service carried chemical tanks from mainland Europe to Dow Chemicals at King's Lynn, which for safety reasons were not allowed to be carried on the same train as Ciba-Geigy's methanol. One solution was to re-route the methanol via Willesden, Doncaster and Whitemoor, adding over 200 miles to the journey.

Another change in 1989 was a new flow of palletised epoxy resins from Monthey in Switzerland to Duxford, initially at the rate of 3,000 tonnes a year. This traffic travelled via the Dunkerque to Dover train ferry.

In addition to its purpose-built and well-used rail facilities at Duxford, Ciba-Geigy continued to receive fuel oil and coal by road from other local railheads. The oil was delivered from Thames Haven to the Charringtons terminal just south of Cambridge station, while the coal came from Daw Mill near Coventry and was offloaded at Cambridge coal concentration depot, also just south of the station.

BR's decision to axe Speedlink in 1991 came as a major blow to Ciba-Geigy. Speedlink offered a flexible daily service with connections to and from all parts of the network. It was ideal for 'spot loads' to unusual destinations, as well as satisfying the customer's preference for 'little and often' or 'just in time' deliveries of raw materials.

Railfreight Distribution and Ciba-Geigy agreed that most of the rail traffic to and from Duxford was ill suited to trainload operation. Small flows such as the china clay from Cornwall would

RAIL FREIGHT: WAGONLOAD

inevitably be transferred to road. Even the outward resin traffic did not produce enough volume on any particular route to warrant trainload operation. BR worked out a draft train plan for the resin to Egger at Hexham, but in the event Egger commissioned its own resin plant near Hexham, then needed to transport only small quantities of a different grade of resin from Duxford.

However, creative solutions were found for keeping the main inward flows of methanol and urea on rail, even though the cost to Ciba-Geigy was an extra £100,000 a year compared with the cheapest road alternative. For the methanol, Ciba-Geigy sponsored a three-times-weekly block train from Purfleet to Duxford, using a Trainload Petroleum locomotive that on the other days of the week worked an oil train from Ripple Lane to Chesterton Junction. In order to mitigate the cost of trainload operation, Ciba-Geigy stopped using the modern Tiphook bogie wagons that had carried the methanol since 1989; instead it reverted to hiring a fleet of 18- to 25-year-old two-axle tank wagons from CAIB.

For the urea, a quasi-wagonload solution was found, using the new daily Railfreight Distribution feeder service for train ferry traffic between Temple Mills and King's Lynn. This train was already booked to call at Duxford on its outward leg for the palletised resin traffic from Switzerland. The empty urea wagons travelled direct from Duxford to King's Lynn, while the loaded wagons travelled from King's Lynn to Temple Mills before returning to Duxford on the following day's train bound for King's Lynn. The extra cost to BR of accommodating the urea was minimal.

Ciba-Geigy remained keen on using rail freight and saw international movements as offering the best hopes of a revival. In particular, it had its eyes on possible import traffic from Pamplona in Spain and on possible export flows to various mainland locations. However, as things turned out even Ciba-Geigy's existing flows came under threat as the costs of using rail rose. The methanol from Purfleet passed to road in April 1993 and the urea from King's Lynn was lost shortly afterwards, BR having withdrawn its service to King's Lynn Docks and cut back its King's Lynn train to terminate at Ely. International traffic continued to use the Duxford terminal for a little longer, but Ciba-Geigy was ultimately forced to admit defeat in its rail freight aspirations.

No 47270 enters Temple Mills yard with the 1330 RfD International service from Kings Lynn on 2 August 1991. The Polybulk wagon behind the locomotive is carrying urea from Kings Lynn Docks to Duxford. The van in front of the locomotive had been left on the reception line by an earlier service and was now being propelled into the yard.

3.

After Speedlink

The closure of Speedlink on 8 July 1991 seemed to be the end of an era for British rail freight. It was as if Beeching had finally been proved right – the future for rail freight lay with bulk traffic in full trainloads, and the time-honoured practice of sorting individual wagons in marshalling yards was dead.

The reality of the Speedlink closure was rather different. BR stated before the withdrawal that it intended to find new arrangements for keeping 50% of former Speedlink tonnages on rail. As things turned out, the retention rate in the first 12 months after July 1991 was nearer to 70%. This was good news for the customers, especially those who had only recently invested in new terminal facilities or rolling-stock. But in railway operational terms the withdrawal from wagonload was not as absolute as BR press releases claimed: some trains continued to convey portions for more than one destination, and limited shunting continued to take place at yards such as Willesden, Warrington Arpley and Mossend.

Essentially the former Speedlink traffic that was retained after July 1991 fell into two categories: traffic to and from mainland Europe, which would continue to be conveyed by a slimmed-down wagonload network, and regular domestic flows, which would be conveyed in dedicated trainloads as far as practicable.

European traffic

For traffic to and from mainland Europe via the Dover-Dunkerque train ferry, Railfreight Distribution ran a dedicated set of trains between Dover and the main industrial centres of Britain, as shown on the map on page 92. Most routes had a daily service from Monday to Friday inclusive, but on the key corridor between Dover and Willesden, RfD ran five trains each way on weekdays as well as additional services at weekends. The trains did not form as flexible a network as Speedlink, as they were designed specifically for flows to and from Dover. However, they could also convey wagons between two inland locations, such as empty ferry vans from a receiving terminal in one part of the country to a forwarding terminal in another area. Conversely, some locations receiving or forwarding ferry traffic were not served directly by the ferry wagon trains; those locations were reached by connecting services operated either by RfD's Chemicals and Industrial Minerals division or by Trainload Freight.

Some sorting of individual ferry wagons took place at Dunkerque and further sorting was carried out at Dover Town yard. Most trains also detached or attached portions at Willesden Brent sidings, from where RfD operated feeder services to and from individual terminals in the South East. One service from Dover to Willesden called at Paddock Wood to detach wagons for the Whirlpool terminal and attach empties for return to Dover via Willesden. RfD operated direct feeder services from Willesden to the general distribution terminals at Neasden, Crawley, Didcot and Cowley, while traffic for locations in East London and East Anglia was conveyed via Temple Mills yard for further sorting.

The Temple Mills pilot locomotive hauled traffic between Temple Mills and London International Freight Terminal (LIFT) at Stratford.

RAIL FREIGHT: WAGONLOAD

Speedlink replacement services, London Midland Region, 1991

Code	Days	Train	Traffic
6A20	SX	0920 Wolverton-Willesden	European
6A49	SO	0905 Corkickle-Willesden	Sodium tripolyphosphate
6B20	SX	0540 Willesden-Wolverton	European
6C12	SO	0240 Ellesmere Port-Plumpton Junc	Chemicals
6C35	SO	0408 Crewe-Sellafield	European
6C49	MO	1320 Sellafield-Carlisle	European
6C51	MSX	0613 Crewe-Carlisle	MoD
6D11	MX	0150 Bescot-Toton	European
6E03	MO	1940 Willesden-Haverton Hill	Carbon dioxide
6E22	TThSO	0430 Spondon-Saltend	Chemicals
6E26	TWFO	1304 Carlisle-Immingham	Fertiliser
6E30	SX	2331 Crewe-Tees	European
6E36	WSO	1244/1030 Carlisle-Port Clarence	Chemicals
6E39	MWFO	0915 Mostyn-Saltend	Chemicals
6E43	MWFO	2015 Baglan Bay-Saltend	Chemicals
6F07	SX	1507 Ordsall Lane-Arpley	European
6F14	SO	0621 Plumpton Junc-Ellesmere Port	Chemicals
6F45	SX	1013 Crewe-Ellesmere Port	European
6F47	SX	1216 Crewe-Garston	European
6G07	SX	1035 Toton-Bescot	European
6G37	SX	1834 Crewe-Lawley Street	MoD
6H64	SX	1958 Crewe-Trafford Park	European and Freightliner
6J15	MX	0340 Crewe-Ordsall Lane	European
6K22	SX	1353 Ellesmere Port-Crewe	European
6K52	MX	0632 Garston-Crewe	European
6K63	SX	1327 Bescot-Longport	European
6K64	SX	2236 Lawley Street-Crewe	MoD
6K65	SX	1721 Longport-Crewe	European
6K73	MX	0415 Trafford Park-Crewe	European and Freightliner
6K84	SX	1532 Preston-Crewe	European and MoD
6K85	SX	1351 Carlisle-Crewe	MoD
6L14	MO	0844 Willesden-West Thurrock	Sodium tripolyphosphate
6L74	SX	0535 Willesden-Temple Mills	European
6M11	SX	0520 Dover-Willesden	European
6M14	SX	1955 Dover-Willesden	European
6M19	SX	0730 Didcot-Fenny Compton	MoD
6M40	MTThO	2120 Immingham-Carlisle	Fertiliser
6M43	SX	1400 Bicester-Lawley Street	MoD
6M48	TO	1844 Haverton Hill-Willesden	Carbon dioxide
6M48	ThSuO	1630 Cameron Bridge-Willesden	Carbon dioxide
6M56	SuO	1945 Dover-Bescot	European
6M57	EWD	0120 Dover-Willesden	European
6M58	WO	1505 Swansea-Dee Marsh Junction	Timber
6M58	SO	1600 Cardiff-Dee Marsh Junction	Timber and chemicals
6M59	ThO	0553 Mossend-Ince	Fertiliser
6M60	MWFO	2050 Falkland Junction-Arpley	Chemicals
6M62	TThSuO	2000 Saltend-Mostyn	Chemicals
6M62	SX	2250 Morris Cowley-Dover	European
6M64	TFO	2050 Port Elphinstone-Willesden	Clay
6M64	MThO	1656 Elgin-Dee Marsh Junction	Timber
6M66	MWFO	2000 Saltend-Spondon	Chemicals
6M73	TThSO	0832 Quidhampton-Willesden	Clay
6M73	SX	1630 Mossend-Crewe	European
6M80	SX	1200 Eastriggs-Carlisle	MoD

AFTER SPEEDLINK

Code	Days	Train	Traffic
6M74	SX	0735 Neasden-Willesden	European
6M74	SX	1100 Glascoed-Crewe	MoD
6M79	SX	1436 Eastleigh-Crewe	MoD
6M82	SX	1735 Temple Mills-Willesden	European
6M86	SX	0850 Dover-Crewe	European
6M87	MWFO	1350 Sheerness-Willesden	Oxygen, clay, starch
6M88	SX	1442 Crawley-Willesden	European
6M89	FO	2120 West Thurrock-Corkickle	Sodium tripolyphosphate
6M89	SX	1530 Scunthorpe-Bescot	European
6M94	SX	1710 Dover-Bescot	European
6M95	TFO	2215 Port Clarence-Carlisle	Chemicals
6N73	SX	0902 Crewe-Blackburn	European and MoD
6O38	MO	0526 Willesden-Dover	European
6O38	MX	0040 Crewe-Dover	European
6O48	TThSO	0523 Willesden-Quidhampton	Clay
6O49	SX	2347 Crewe-Eastleigh	MoD
6O56	SX	1920 Cardiff-Dover	European
6O63	SX	1133 Willesden-Crawley	European
6O76	MWFO	0855 Willesden-Sheerness	Oxygen, clay, starch
6O97	EWD	0030 Bescot-Dover	European
6O98	SX	1319 Willesden-Dover	European
6O99	SX	2145 Willesden-Dover	European
6S56	SX	1030 Carlisle-Eastriggs	MoD
6S61	TThSuO	2300 Arpley-Falkland Junction	Chemicals
6S67	MWFO	0452 St Blazey-Mossend	Various
6S69	WSuO	2206 Dee Marsh Junction-Elgin	Timber
6S70	SX	0810 Crewe-Mossend	European
6S71	MO	2256 Ince-Mossend	Fertiliser
6S72	MThO	2100 Willesden-Port Elphinstone	Clay
6S85	WFO	1940 Willesden-Cameron Bridge	Carbon dioxide
6T64	SX	1130 Blackburn-Preston via Bamber Bridge and Chorley	European and MoD
6T68	MWFO	1000 Arpley-Newton-le-Willows	Carbon dioxide
6T68	MWFO	1115 Newton-le-Willows-Arpley	Carbon dioxide
6T68	TThSO	0630 Arpley-Folly Lane	Chemicals
6T68	TThSO	0910 Folly Lane-Arpley via Middlewich and Sandbach	Chemicals
6T68	TThO	1405 Arpley-St Helens	Chemicals
6T68	TThO	1615 St Helens-Arpley	Chemicals
6T68	TThO	1800 Arpley-Ellesmere Port	Chemicals
6T68	TThO	1930 Ellesmere Port-Arpley	Chemicals
6T69	SO	0900 Arpley-St Helens	Chemicals
6T69	SO	1105 St Helens-Arpley	Chemicals
6T71	SO	0830 Arpley-Ellesmere Port	Chemicals
6T71	SO	1045 Ellesmere Port-Arpley	Chemicals
6T92	WO	1355 Llandudno Junction-Holyhead	European
6T92	WO	1725 Holyhead-Llandudno Junction	European
6T95	MWFO	1000 Crewe-Radway Green	MoD
6T95	MWFO	1145 Radway Green-Crewe	MoD
6V01	SX	0545 Willesden-Neasden	European
6V03	SX	1000 Fenny Compton-Didcot	MoD
6V12	SX	0325 Crewe-Glascoed	MoD
6V14	MWFO	0800 Saltend-Baglan Bay	Chemicals
6V16	SX	1037 Willesden-Morris Cowley	European
6V19	SX	1900 Lawley Street-Didcot	MoD
6V20	TO	1435 Dee Marsh Junction-Carmarthen	Timber
6V20	FO	1435 Dee Marsh Junction-Cardiff	Timber and chemicals
6V88	MX	0130 Willesden-Cardiff	European
6V93	TThSO	0523 Mossend-St Blazey	Various

RAIL FREIGHT: WAGONLOAD

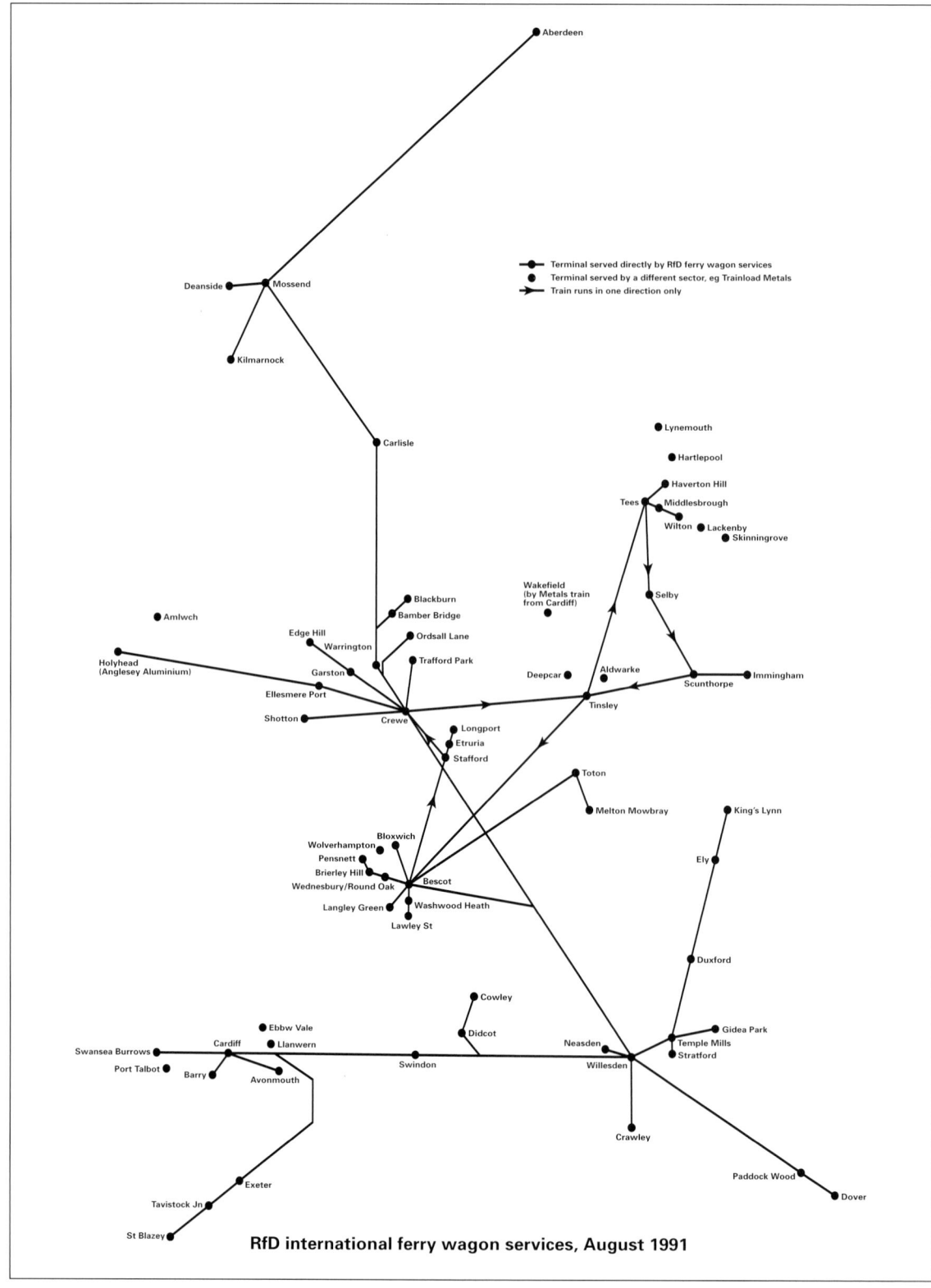

AFTER SPEEDLINK

Above Speedlink-style operations survived after July 1991 on routes served by RfD's European trains. With a well-mixed train in tow, No 47033 passes Selby station with 6D36, the 0828 service from Tees Yard to Scunthorpe, on 18 July 1991. The train has already called at the Potter distribution depot on the east side of Selby and will shortly shunt the Viking Shipping terminal in Selby station goods yard. After arrival at Scunthorpe the train will continue to Tinsley, then Bescot, connecting with an overnight service to Dover.

Below The trunk European services to and from Dover were often well loaded; the catch, as with all wagonload traffic, was the need to run separate trip workings, which often conveyed only a handful of wagons. No 58008 provides unusual traction for 6M86, the 0850 from Dover to Bescot, pictured at Atherstone on 24 July 1991.

Civilink resources were used to convey train ferry traffic on certain routes. On 31 July 1992 No 37023 leaves Peterborough with a single IZA van for the Potter Group terminal at Ely, running as 6L60, the 1054 from Peterborough to March.

Two further connecting trains operated out of Temple Mills: one served the Railstore distribution depot at Gidea Park, and the other ran to King's Lynn. The latter train conveyed chemicals for Duxford (Ciba-Geigy) and King's Lynn (Dow Chemicals), as well as general merchandise to and from the Potter Group distribution depot at Ely. This train also carried a domestic flow of urea from King's Lynn to Duxford, with the loaded wagons running via Temple Mills and the 'empties' conveyed direct.

Ferry wagon traffic to and from South Wales and South West England was conveyed by overnight services from Willesden to Cardiff and from Cardiff to Dover. At Cardiff, RfD shared the use of Tidal yard with Trainload Freight. This meant that RfD traffic from South Wales steel plants such as Port Talbot and Llanwern could be brought to Tidal yard by Trainload Metals services and feed directly into RfD's train to Dover without any further 'tripping'. RfD operated its own trip workings from Cardiff to Swansea Burrows, Barry and Avonmouth, and ran a daily train between Cardiff and South West England for the considerable volume of bagged and bulk china clay that was exported via Dover. The clay was brought to St Blazey and Tavistock Junction yards by trip workings sponsored by RfD Chemicals and Industrial Minerals.

Bescot yard was the centre of RfD operations in the West Midlands. RfD operated its own trip workings to most terminals handling ferry wagons, but Trainload Metals trips carried RfD traffic between Bescot and Wolverhampton. As in all parts of the system, RfD was careful to make the best possible use of resources: European chemicals traffic for Langley Green, for example, was carried between Bescot and Langley Green by the train that conveyed domestic chemicals from Teesside to Langley Green, so the European traffic did not require an extra locomotive or crew.

An intensive diagram from Bescot served all ferry wagon terminals in the East and North Midlands. In the early hours of the morning it ran to Toton, where it detached vanloads of petfood for Melton Mowbray, and, after returning to Bescot by lunchtime, it headed north to Stafford

AFTER SPEEDLINK

and the Potteries. From the Potteries the train ran forward to Crewe instead of returning to Bescot, so that it could connect with the overnight Crewe-Dover service. The main traffic flows on the Potteries leg of this diagram were packaged chemicals to Stafford for Grilon, steel from British Steel Shelton (Etruria) and general merchandise to Longport freight depot.

All ferry wagon traffic to and from Crewe and beyond was conveyed by a daily trunk train between Dover and Crewe, where Basford Hall sidings came back into use for sorting wagonload freight for the first time since 1972. Traffic for North West England was taken forward from Crewe by separate trip workings, some of which were shared with other divisions of RfD. Ferry traffic for Trafford Park, for example, used one of the scheduled Freightliner services between Crewe and Trafford Park, while ferry traffic for Merseyside was conveyed by an RfD locomotive using marginal time between Freightliner duties. Chemicals for export from Amlwch were carried by the daily Amlwch-Ellesmere Port chemicals train, and the locomotive from that service also made two weekly trips from Llandudno Junction to Holyhead and back, carrying BR fuel oil to Holyhead and aluminium for export from Anglesea Aluminium.

RfD operated two further trunk trains each weekday from Crewe. One served North East England and Yorkshire, visiting Tinsley yard, Tees yard, Selby, Scunthorpe, Tinsley yard and finally Bescot. By starting this train at Crewe and terminating it at Bescot, RfD was able to balance the locomotive roster with the East Midlands service, which started at Bescot and terminated at Crewe. The North East train carried a wide range of flows, including steel products that were transported between individual terminals and Tinsley and Tees yards by Trainload Metals resources. At Selby the train called at two privately owned distribution depots for train ferry traffic, one operated by the Potter Group on the sugar factory site and the other managed by Viking Shipping in the former station goods yard. At Scunthorpe further steel wagons were attached, including traffic from Immingham. Ferry wagon traffic to and from Wakefield Cobra distribution terminal was, however, conveyed by a Trainload Metals service between Cardiff and Wakefield.

The BR freight terminal at Longport managed to escape the cull of railway-owned goods depots that accompanied the demise of Speedlink. Pilot locomotive No 08599 shunts IWA ferry vans at Longport after the arrival of the daily feeder service from Bescot on 5 August 1991.

The daytime RfD European service from Mossend to Crewe carried specific flows of domestic traffic as well as ferry wagons. No 90149 passes Acton Grange Junction with 6M53, the 0800 departure from Mossend, on 10 July 1992. The load includes one Cerestar JIA tank returning from Aberdeen to Trafford Park and four KFA container wagons returning from Deanside to Melton Mowbray.

The second trunk ferry wagon service from Crewe ran to Mossend and catered for all Scottish traffic. Bottled whisky from Deanside and Kilmarnock and paper from Aberdeen were among the main flows carried on this service. The train also had enough capacity for some domestic traffic, including Guinness beer from Park Royal to Deanside and empty wagons returning to Melton Mowbray after carrying petfood to Deanside. The connection to Aberdeen was initially provided by an RfD intermodal service from Mossend and Coatbridge to Aberdeen and Elgin, launched on 9 July 1991 for an experimental period of two years. However, the intermodal business failed to become established.

RfD constantly reviewed its services for train ferry traffic, conscious of the need to maintain customer confidence in the run-up to the opening of the Channel Tunnel, but also eager to minimise its financial losses. In 1992 it withdrew some lightly loaded feeder services such as those to Crawley and Edge Hill and reduced the frequency of several other feeder services in order to allow the sharing of resources between two services. From Warrington, for example, one feeder service now operated either to Ordsall Lane or to Blackburn. RfD recast its service to Yorkshire and Teesside by re-routing the trunk train via Toton, Selby and Scunthorpe, allowing the withdrawal of the separate train between Bescot and Toton. Any ferry wagon traffic to and from Teesside, such as imported steel for Middlesbrough, would now use an RfD chemicals train from Warrington to Port Clarence. On the positive side, RfD responded to heavy loadings between South Wales and mainland Europe by introducing a second daily service between Cardiff, Llanwern and Willesden. In 1993 RfD made further changes, such as withdrawing from Temple Mills yard and cutting the service frequency to Gidea Park and Ely from daily to three times weekly on each route.

Domestic traffic: 'contract trains' and Tiger Freightways

For domestic ex-Speedlink flows, RfD made agreements with individual customers from July 1991 to run block trains between specific terminals. These were known as 'contract trains' and generally ran for the benefit of a single customer. However, in a few cases one train was shared by two or more customers. The shared workings incurred the costs of shunting and tripping similar to those that had been the downfall of Speedlink.

RfD retained nearly all the chemical flows that had been conveyed by Speedlink. The BP Chemicals plant at Saltend was the main source of Speedlink traffic in the Hull area, and this traffic was re-organised into regular block trains serving Mostyn (via Ellesmere Port), Baglan Bay, Spondon and Seal Sands. Chlorine traffic from Wilton to Langley Green had already been formed into a block train before the end of Speedlink, but this service now carried other chemicals from Teesside to the West Midlands, such as carbon dioxide from Haverton Hill to Coleshill. RfD also provided a twice-weekly service for carbon dioxide from Cameron Bridge and Mossend to Warrington

The first working of 6M64, the 1656 Elgin to Dee Marsh Junction timber train, passes Daresbury on 9 July 1991 behind Nos 37261 and 37262, conveying 34 OTA wagons for the Shotton Paper Company.

Arpley, from where wagons were tripped to Newton-le-Willows, and Willesden.

From Warrington RfD operated a number of trip workings. The locomotive that tripped the carbon dioxide to and from Newton-le-Willows also collected chemicals traffic as required from Sandbach, Middlewich, Runcorn, St Helens and Ellesmere Port. Most of the traffic from the last five locations was combined into a three-times-weekly service to Carlisle yard, for tripping to British Sidac at Wigton, and Falkland yard, for delivery to ICI at Stevenston and Roche Products at Dalry. At Carlisle this train connected with a twice-weekly chemicals working from Port Clarence. In early 1993 RfD combined the flows from Cheshire and the North East to Dalry into a single train, running from Warrington and calling for traffic purposes at Port Clarence only.

RfD scheduled two block chemicals services for Saturdays-only operation, using resources that would otherwise be standing idle. They were a weekly trainload of caustic soda and other chemicals from Ellesmere Port to the Glaxo plant at Plumpton Junction and a weekly trainload of sodium tripolyphosphate from Corkickle to West Thurrock for Albright & Wilson. The change from daily to weekly operation from Corkickle forced the customer to invest in additional wagons. The Plumpton Junction train was later extended to Sellafield to convey nitric acid from Ince & Elton for British Nuclear Fuels.

In East Anglia Ciba-Geigy at Duxford received a three-times-weekly trainload of methanol from Purfleet, in addition to the wagonload deliveries of urea from King's Lynn conveyed by the European train. Those flows continued until 1993.

The fertiliser plants at Immingham (Norsk Hydro) and Ince & Elton (Kemira) had in the past produced a mixture of trainload and wagonload traffic. Some of the wagonload flows from those plants were incorporated into new contract trains. From Immingham block trains ran to Carlisle and Aberdeen, using the same resources that covered existing block trains to Avonmouth and Leith. New destinations for contract trains from Ince & Elton were Diss, Lugton and Thornton. The Diss train took the path of the now withdrawn train to Crawley, still detaching traffic for Akeman Street at Bletchley. The traffic to Lugton and Thornton was conveyed in a single weekly train from Ince & Elton to Mossend.

Above The Albright & Wilson works at Oldbury continued to receive wagonload deliveries of phosphorus from mainland Europe as well as chlorine from Wilton. No 47345 shunts the Oldbury terminal on 23 July 1991 while working 6T48 from Bescot.

Below Chemicals traffic on the Cumbrian Coast line was carried by two Saturdays-only trains, one serving Corkickle and the other Sellafield and Plumpton Junction. No 37026 passes Plumpton Junction exchange sidings with 6F14, the 1028 Sellafield to Ellesmere Port train, on 27 February 1993. The load comprises two empty nitric acid tanks from Sellafield to Ince & Elton and four empty tank wagons from Plumpton Junction to Ellesmere Port. The wagons from Plumpton Junction had been collected on the outward journey of this train from Ellesmere Port to Sellafield.

AFTER SPEEDLINK

BR managed to retain nearly all the china clay traffic that had been carried by Speedlink. Most of the domestic flows were taken over by Tiger Rail, which sponsored wagonload services from Cornwall and Salisbury to the Potteries, Glasgow and North East Scotland. The service from Cornwall to Cliffe Vale in the Potteries had operated since the introduction of air-braked wagons in 1982 and now continued much as before under Tiger Rail management. On the other routes, Tiger Rail took the more radical step of offering a wagonload service for any available traffic between the points served, in other words a like-for-like replacement for Speedlink. The service was marketed as Tiger Freightways. With this service the company hoped not only to retain former Speedlink flows but also to attract new traffic and to expand its operation to other routes.

The most heavily used Tiger Freightways train, regularly loading to 90% of its booked capacity, was the three-times-weekly working from St Blazey to Mossend, carrying china clay from several loading points in the South West to receiving terminals at Warrington, Mossend, Auchmuty, Corpach, Aberdeen and Port Elphinstone, as well as cider from Taunton to Mossend, electrical goods from Bodmin to Warrington and Mossend, and calcified seaweed from Drinnick Mill to Mossend and Carlisle. The traffic to Carlisle was detached from the Tiger Freightways train at Warrington and continued its journey on a Civilink engineers' train from Warrington to Carlisle.

The St Blazey to Mossend train connected at Mossend with a three-times-weekly Tiger Freightways service from Quidhampton and Willesden to Aberdeen and Port Elphinstone.

No 90038 passes Holme with 6V92, the 0523 Mossend to St Blazey Tiger Freightways service, on 13 July 1991. The load consists of two PAAs from Markinch to Goonbarrow, one TTA from Corpach to Burngullow, one IRB from Mossend to Parkandillack, one JIA from Mossend to St Blazey, one TUA from Mossend to Burngullow, and three IZAs from Mossend to Taunton.

No 86639 approaches Leighton Buzzard with 6M64, the 2050 Port Elphinstone to Willesden Tiger Freightways service, on 28 August 1991. The first three wagons are TUA and TCA tanks with calcium carbonate slurry from Aberdeen Waterloo to Sittingbourne, followed by empty ICA tanks returning from Port Elphinstone to Quidhampton.

RAIL FREIGHT: WAGONLOAD

No 47206 arrives at Sittingbourne with 6O76, the 0855 Willesden to Sheerness service, on 2 August 1991. The consist includes one TUA tank with calcium carbonate from Aberdeen to Sittingbourne, one TCA and one TBA with calcium carbonate from Quidhampton to Sittingbourne, two PCA tanks with starch from Trafford Park to Sittingbourne and two TEA tanks with liquid oxygen from Ditton to Sheerness. The calcium carbonate will be discharged in the shed visible behind the train, while the starch will be unloaded in the goods yard at the other end of the station.

This service carried calcium carbonate slurry to Port Elphinstone as well as calcium carbonate slurry from Quidhampton to Sittingbourne and chalk slurry from Aberdeen to Sittingbourne. The Willesden to Sittingbourne link was covered by a further Tiger Freightways service, also conveying flows of oxygen from Ditton to Sheerness and starch from Trafford Park to Sittingbourne, which reached Willesden on RfD services. Finally, Tiger ran a twice-weekly train from Furzebrook and Eastleigh to Bescot, conveying ball clay from Furzebrook to Cliffe Vale.

Unfortunately, the Tiger Freightways venture did not last long. The company's holding group went into receivership in February 1992 and its embryonic wagonload network faced an uncertain future. Negotiation between RfD and Tiger's former wagonload customers produced a rescue plan for the long-distance services from the South West to Cliffe Vale and from Quidhampton to Port Elphinstone. However, it was not possible to save the St Blazey to Mossend service, despite its healthy loadings. The clay flows to Mossend and Auchmuty were lost, while clay from the South West to Corpach and Aberdeen was rerouted using the Cliffe Vale train as far as Bescot, then RfD European services from Bescot to Crewe and from Crewe to Mossend, and finally RfD services from Mossend to Corpach and Aberdeen. For Taunton Cider RfD introduced a weekly block train from Taunton to Mossend, which also carried lighting products from Bodmin. However, in December 1992 RfD was unable to renegotiate terms with Taunton Cider and the Taunton to Mossend service ceased.

The Ministry of Defence had been a significant user of Speedlink services and for strategic reasons wished to keep as much traffic on rail as possible. RfD established a mini-network for the MoD, with a daily trunk service on the main corridor between Eastleigh, Didcot, Crewe and Carlisle and scheduled trip workings to and from the busiest depots, including Marchwood, Ludgershall, Bicester, Kineton, Longtown and Eastriggs. RfD would run special trains as required to less busy depots such as Long Marston and Glen Douglas. However, it was not practicable to retain a service to some of the remoter MoD locations such as Crombie, Trecwn and Ernesettle.

Agricultural lime presented something of a challenge for RfD because of its seasonal nature and because of the small tonnages on offer between any given pair of locations. However, it found a combined trainload solution for two of the main flows of lime, from Thrislington to Inverurie and from Ferryhill to Montrose. Tiger Rail expressed an interest in taking over this train and opening it up to other potential wagonload flows between North East England and North East Scotland; however, these plans were overtaken by Tiger's demise.

Raw timber had been a major growth area in the Speedlink era, but the need to collect small quantities from a large number of railheads made

Above No 37101 passes South Moreton with 6M79, the 1436 Eastleigh to Crewe Ministry of Defence train, on 31 July 1991. The wagons had reached Eastleigh on feeder services from Marchwood and Ludgershall, and at Didcot further traffic will be added from Kineton and Bicester.

Below A single VGA van forms 6A49, the 1225 MoD feeder service from Didcot to Bicester, on 30 August 1991. The traction is No 37194, at that time a member of the nationwide pool of Class 37s nominally based at Tinsley.

Above In 1992 the Central Ordnance Depot at Bicester was one of only two national storage and distribution centres for all kinds of military supplies, handling everything from vehicle spares and ironmongery to Army uniforms and camouflage nets. Its 43 miles of track were used mainly for internal movements, but also handled traffic to and from other military depots in a mixture of railway-owned and MoD-owned wagons. One of the five pilot locomotives based on the site, 'Steelman' 0-4-0 No 276, leads a rake of VGA vans past one of the Graven Hill traffic sheds on 21 July.

Below RfD provided an intermodal train between Didcot and Cardiff Pengam Freightliner terminal for military traffic to and from South Wales. It continued to run under EWS management and was diverted to Wentloog in 2001. No 37707 approaches East Usk Junction with 4B24, the 1550 Didcot to Pengam train, on 16 July 1997.

AFTER SPEEDLINK

most timber flows uneconomic. The only customer to receive timber by rail immediately after July 1991 was the Shotton Paper Company. Contract trains ran to Shotton from North East Scotland, South Wales and South West England, with one pair of locomotives making two return trips to Elgin, one to Cardiff and one to Carmarthen each week. Timber from Exeter used a connecting service to Cardiff.

Another growth area in Speedlink days was canned drinks traffic, but this too proved difficult to transfer to block train operation. The two firms that continued to use rail were Taunton Cider, as mentioned above, and Guinness, who sent five block trains a week from Park Royal to the Otis distribution terminal at Ordsall Lane, Salford. The Guinness contract justified the building of additional rail sidings and a second transhipment shed at Ordsall Lane, from where the traffic was distributed by road to all parts of northern England and North Wales. The Guinness train from Park Royal also conveyed traffic for Glasgow Deanside, which was detached at Crewe and carried forward on RfD's European train.

Grain traffic was difficult to salvage because of its seasonal and disparate nature. RfD managed to schedule a service conveying Polybulk wagons from Kings Lynn and Eccles Road to Roseisle and Burghead, but it only lasted one season. Molasses continued to travel by rail until 1993, with block trains operating as required from several terminals in eastern England to Menstrie.

Automotive flows were only marginally affected by the demise of Speedlink. On some routes such as Merseyside to South Wales Speedlink trains carrying automotive traffic were superseded by automotive contract trains running between the same points. However, Ford cars from Merseyside to Exeter were conveyed in less-than-trainload quantities, using a Garston to Bridgend automotive service as far as East Usk Junction and a connecting train from East Usk Junction to Exeter.

Most wagonload cement traffic was transferred to Trainload Construction's own services before

Grain traffic made a short-lived return to rail after the end of Speedlink. No 47297 approaches Greenhill Lower Junction on 16 April 1992 with 6H40, the 0950 Thursdays-only contract train from Mossend to Inverness. The traffic was bound for Burghead and Roseisle. The eight Polybulk wagons were the maximum permitted load for a Class 47-hauled train on the Highland main line; four further Polybulk wagons had been detached at Mossend and would make their way north on the Mossend to Elgin intermodal train.

the end of Speedlink, so this underwent little change in July 1991. The only building materials traffic that became an RfD contract service was that carrying Plasmor blocks from Heck to three terminals in the South East. A daily train ran from Heck to Biggleswade and Temple Mills (for Bow), also calling at Peterborough to detach traffic for Wymondham. The connection from Peterborough to Wymondham was scheduled to run two days a week.

The Speedlink network had been used to carry diesel fuel – 'gas oil' in railway parlance – to most locomotive and DMU fuelling points on BR. Some of this traffic was transferred to Trainload Petroleum services in the late 1980s, but the majority of flows continued to use Speedlink until July 1991. After that, Trainload Petroleum found creative solutions for a number of fuelling points, some of which were not easily reached by road. Gas oil from Stanlow to Buxton, for example, was carried by a Trainload Petroleum service from Stanlow to Ditton, then by a Trainload Construction service from Ditton to Peak Forest, and finally by local arrangement from Peak Forest to Buxton. Trainload Petroleum also made its own arrangements for the small number of commercial flows that were carried by Speedlink until July 1991, including Harwich to Longport for Carless, and Fawley to Cambridge Coldhams Lane for Flitwick Oil Services.

Enterprise

The decision to axe Speedlink in 1991 not only alienated some existing rail freight customers, especially those who had invested in new facilities, but also prevented potential customers from trying out rail freight without committing themselves to sponsoring a full trainload. In 1994 the Rail Freight Group (RFG) carried out market research among a large number of existing and potential rail freight users to see what use they would be prepared to make of a revived less-than-trainload network. In contrast to BR's earlier survey, RFG found that there was enough traffic on offer on several key routes to justify a regular less-than-trainload service.

At the same time, Trainload Freight was being prepared for privatisation and was divided between the three 'companies' Transrail, Loadhaul and Mainline Freight. Transrail covered a wider geographical area than the other two companies and inherited most of those former Speedlink flows that had been recast into trainload movements. It was these factors, coupled with Transrail's new entrepreneurial spirit, that led to the setting up of Transrail's less-than-trainload network, Enterprise.

The Enterprise service was officially unveiled to customers by Transrail Managing Director Julian Worth at the company launch in Warrington on 5 September 1994. A series of roadshow meetings followed, where customers were told that Transrail would move as little as 50 tonnes a day over a suitable distance – a far cry from the 1,000 tonnes generally required to fill a trainload. Enterprise was dubbed the 'rail motorway' and its aim was to take 100,000 lorry journeys off Britain's roads in its first year. Not surprisingly, Enterprise was warmly welcomed by environmental groups such as Transport 2000, as well as by customers such as Cerestar, which had struggled to keep its business on rail after the end of Speedlink.

The first scheduled Enterprise trains ran between Mossend and Willesden on 26 September 1994. The timetable also included trunk services between Warrington and Teesside, between Bescot and Newport Alexandra Dock Junction, and between St Blazey and Cliffe Vale. Connecting services were provided from Mossend to Inverness, Elgin, Huntly, Inverurie, Aberdeen, Cameron Bridge, Thornton, Millerhill, Corpach, Fort William, Deanside and Dalry, from Tees Yard to Middlesbrough Goods, from Warrington to Carlisle, Workington, Sellafield, Castleton, St Helens, Trafford Park, Ditton, Runcorn, Ince & Elton, Shotton, Middlewich and Sandbach, from Bescot to Coleshill and Washwood Heath, from Newport to Swansea, and from Willesden to Quidhampton, Sittingbourne and Sheerness.

To begin with, most of the traffic was former Speedlink business that had switched to contract train operation or – in the case of Cerestar – to RfD European services. Customers welcomed the restored flexibility of a daily service where they had previously had to adapt to just one or two trains a week. Wagon turnround times were improved on flows such as timber from North East

AFTER SPEEDLINK

Scotland to Shotton. And Transrail was able to provide the Enterprise trains with no significant increase in costs: it was largely a case of making existing contract trains available to other customers. The company could even achieve economies on some routes by combining two existing flows into a single train.

Enterprise soon began to attract new traffic. An early example was Co-Steel at Sheerness. Transrail had inherited a three-times-weekly service between Willesden and Sheerness, but this conveyed only liquid oxygen to the Co-Steel plant as well as china clay and starch to Sittingbourne. Outgoing steel traffic from Sheerness had ceased because Trainload Metals was only interested in moving regular trainloads and the Sheerness traffic on offer did not fit this pattern. However, the setting up of Enterprise brought the possibility of a more flexible service. An initial consignment of 1,000 tonnes to Mossend was followed by further deliveries to Mossend, Blackburn, Wakefield, Burton-on-Trent and Warrington.

The Mossend terminal used for Co-Steel traffic was already served by the trunk Anglo-Scottish Enterprise train and the steel could therefore be carried at minimal extra cost. Blackburn could be served by sharing an existing Railfreight Distribution service between Crewe and Blackburn, with an additional call at Warrington to intersect with the Enterprise network. Wakefield was served by an intermediate call on the daily Enterprise service from Warrington to Teesside. And Burton-on-Trent could be served by using the existing Transrail departmental service between Bescot and Burton-on-Trent wagon repair shops. Transrail solved the possible problem of finding suitable wagons for the Co-Steel traffic by using former SPA and BDA revenue-earning wagons that had been transferred to departmental use. The Co-Steel business soon grew sufficiently for Transrail to increase the frequency of the Sheerness train from three to five times a week.

Another new traffic flow for Enterprise was domestic and industrial coal from Gascoigne Wood near Selby to distribution points at Mossend, Elgin and Aberdeen. In this instance the volume was large enough for Transrail to run a new feeder service from Gascoigne Wood to Warrington, connecting with scheduled Enterprise services to Scotland. The customer, British Fuels, was able to redeploy wagons and containers that had previously carried coal for export to Ireland for Cawoods.

A similar combination of Enterprise and contract train services enabled the flow of tinplate from Ebbw Vale to Wisbech to return to rail. Transrail conveyed this traffic by combining a metals train from Ebbw Vale to Alexandra Dock Junction, Enterprise services from Alexandra Dock Junction to Warrington, and the Spillers Deanside-Wisbech train from Warrington to Wisbech.

In January 1997 EWS combined several different flows into a single Enterprise train between Warrington and Teesside. No 56123 passes Healey Mills yard with 6E41, the 1205 Warrington Arpley to Lackenby working, on 26 August 1998. The load includes empty steel carriers returning from Blackburn to Lackenby, empty carbon dioxide tanks returning to Haverton Hill, and loaded steel carriers from South Wales to Wakefield.

Burton-on-Trent became a busy rail freight location with intermodal and steel traffic in the early 2000s. No 66098 reverses into the down sidings with 6D36, the 0555 departure from Bescot, on 23 July 2004, conveying five French-registered IHA steel carriers.

A small-scale flow that would have been unthinkable without Enterprise was scrap metal from Aberdeen to Ayr Harbour, amounting to just one wagon a week. Enterprise already operated a regular service between Aberdeen and Ayr via Mossend yard, so the scrap could be carried at virtually no extra cost. Further new flows that plugged straight into the Enterprise network in its early days were starch from Trafford Park to Thornton, steel rail from Workington to Tees Dock for export, caustic soda from Ellesmere Port to Sellafield, and china clay slurry from Burngullow to Mossend.

Among the other flows that Transrail gained in the first 12 months of Enterprise, some of them on a short-term or trial basis only, were calcified seaweed from Truro to Carlisle, calcium carbonate from Quidhampton to Workington, fertiliser from Ince & Elton to Carmarthen, scrap metal from Ashburys to Tees Dock, steel from Cardiff to Sittingbourne, steel from Cardiff to Warrington, and timber from Fort William to Workington.

However, not every former Speedlink flow was suitable for revival through Enterprise. The once buoyant rail traffic from Taunton Cider looked promising because Taunton lay on an existing Enterprise route, but it stayed on road partly because Transrail could not serve the required destinations – including Holyhead and Stranraer – economically. Similarly Kronospan at Chirk did not resume rail movements in Transrail days because its timber came from East Anglia, which had no Enterprise service.

In January 1995 Transrail introduced a second overnight train between Warrington and Mossend to supplement the original trunk service between Willesden, Bescot, Warrington and Mossend. Within a few months the company regained the former Speedlink flow of glassworks lime from Dowlow to Mossend. Further growth in 1995 included a new trunk Enterprise between Alexandra Dock Junction and Warrington, which catered for a variety of traffic including tinplate

Right **Enterprise traffic built up quickly on the West Coast Main Line between Warrington and Mossend, justifying a twice-daily service from January 1995. No 60015 crosses the River Esk at Mossband, north of Carlisle, with 6M27, the 1448 Mossend to Willesden train, on 24 February 1995. The traffic comprises empty salt hoppers from Dalry to Runcorn, empty chemical tanks from Dalry to Port Clarence, one empty Cerestar starch wagon returning to Trafford Park, and loaded carbon dioxide tanks from Cameron Bridge to Willesden.**

RAIL FREIGHT: WAGONLOAD

Britain's newest marshalling yard, Wembley European Freight Operations Centre, was completed in 1993 as the main gathering point in Britain for Channel Tunnel traffic. The yard is pictured on 22 July 1999 with a typical assortment of intermodal and conventional wagons. By that time it was handling domestic traffic that had previously been dealt with at Willesden Brent sidings as well as traffic to and from mainland Europe.

services. However, the overnight Bescot to Sittingbourne Enterprise service continued to call at Willesden Brent to detach wagonloads of carbon dioxide for the adjacent Distillers terminal.

Additional trip workings around London for new Enterprise flows included services from Wembley to Gidea Park, Purfleet and Tilbury. The Gidea Park terminal had been a casualty of RfD cutbacks in 1996 but was now once again able to handle Connectrail traffic in addition to new Enterprise flows. Purfleet dispatched regular container-loads of aviation fuel to Georgemas Junction for Wick airport, while the Tilbury train conveyed mainly imported chemical pulp destined for Workington.

North Kent continued to be fertile ground for Enterprise. The service to and from Sittingbourne and Sheerness was increased to twice daily in June 1997. In order to avoid unnecessary marshalling, and because most wagons from North Kent were destined for the Midlands and North, the departing service from Sheerness ran through to Bescot without calling at Willesden or Wembley en route. The corresponding southbound service called at Willesden to set down only.

In the West Midlands, the concentration of most Connectrail services on Bescot instead of Washwood Heath yard in June 1997 assured easier connections between Connectrail and Enterprise services. However, RfD's feeder services from Bescot to Longport and from Bescot to Aldwarke, Wakefield and Rotherham continued to run exclusively for Connectrail traffic for the time being.

In South Wales and the South West, two major changes took place in June 1997. First, EWS catered for heavy loadings to northern England by running a second daily service between Avonmouth, Newport and Warrington. The

AFTER SPEEDLINK

that made good use of the fast service was paper from Aberdeen to Northampton in prototype Roadrailer bi-modal vehicles.

A conventional wagon flow that used the 75mph train was bottled mineral water from Inverness, loaded in VBA vans and destined for distribution depots at Blackburn, Avonmouth, Ely and Gidea Park. The service also conveyed Scottish Connectrail traffic such as paper from Aberdeen to France. Unlike other Enterprise trains on the West Coast Main Line, the 75mph service was electrically hauled throughout, using a Class 90 locomotive hired from RfD pending the sale of RfD to EWS.

A further example of shared operation between EWS and RfD was the revised nightly service between Carlisle and Eastleigh. Previously this route was covered by RfD services between Carlisle and Crewe Basford Hall and between Crewe Basford Hall and Eastleigh, running exclusively for the Ministry of Defence. From June 1997 the service called at Bescot instead of Basford Hall and, although still sponsored by RfD, was available to carry EWS flows as well as MoD traffic. Examples of the EWS flows conveyed by this train were pulp from Sheerness to Workington on the Bescot to Carlisle leg, and calcium carbonate from Quidhampton to Scotland on the Eastleigh to Bescot leg.

The Eastleigh link created further business opportunities for EWS in the Hampshire area, and an intermediate call at Didcot catered for traffic to and from Didcot Milton distribution centre, which had seen little rail traffic since the 1980s. The Didcot call also allowed interchange of wagons with the nightly RfD service between Alexandra Dock Junction and Wembley.

EWS made a number of changes to Enterprise operations in the London area in June 1997. It transferred most Enterprise marshalling from Willesden Brent yard to the RfD-owned Wembley European Freight Operations Centre. This change brought the obvious advantage of an easier interface between Enterprise and Connectrail

No 56031 pulls out of Alexandra Dock Junction yard, Newport, with 6M14, the 1740 Connectrail departure to Wembley, on 15 July 1997. The first two wagons are IRB Polybulk hoppers returning empty to Château-Feuillet after carrying silicon to Barry. This train was still classed as Connectrail rather than Enterprise, but had recently switched from RfD Class 47 to EWS Class 56 haulage.

No 56069 arrives at Immingham reception sidings with 6G44, the 1508 trip working from Grimsby Docks, on 7 August 2002. The load comprises VKA, VGA and VAA vans with imported zinc ingots for Trident Alloys, Bloxwich.

savings as it replaced three separate trains: the three-times-weekly Enterprise service between Warrington and Tees Yard, a three-times-weekly block steel train between Lackenby and Blackburn, and an Enterprise feeder service between Warrington and Blackburn. The revised train also carried a new flow of steel coil from Port Talbot and Llanwern to Wakefield.

EWS opened up South Humberside to Enterprise traffic by diverting the daily train between Immingham and Wolverhampton Steel Terminal to run via the West Midlands hub at Bescot instead of via Washwood Heath. This change enabled EWS to carry wagonloads of imported zinc from Grimsby to Bloxwich, where it joined the long-established Connectrail flow from Budel in the Netherlands.

In South East England, EWS consolidated Transrail's gain of finished steel traffic out of Sheerness. The North Kent feeder service also started to convey wagonloads of pulp from Sheerness to Workington for Iggesund Paperboard, as well as steel and other traffic to and from the recently established Victa Railfreight terminal at Sittingbourne.

South West England benefited from a new daily Enterprise working in January 1997 between Alexandra Dock Junction and St Blazey, calling at Hallen Marsh, Exeter and Tavistock Junction. The principal traffic on this train was coal from South Wales to Tavistock Junction for Plymstock cement works. It also conveyed other flows such as lead shot from Falmouth, calcified seaweed from Truro and electrical goods from Bodmin.

The timetable change of June 1997 brought the biggest shake-up of the Enterprise network since its launch, partly as a result of continued traffic growth and partly because EWS was in the throes of acquiring RfD and wanted to reap the benefits of integrating the Enterprise and Connectrail networks as quickly as possible.

The busiest Enterprise route remained the West Coast corridor linking London, the West Midlands, North West England and central Scotland. In June 1997 EWS expanded the service to three trains daily in each direction between Wembley and Warrington, five between Warrington and Carlisle and four between Carlisle and Mossend.

The flagship West Coast train was now a 75mph service, running nightly in both directions between Wembley and Mossend and making intermediate calls at Daventry and Warrington Arpley. The scheduled transit time between Wembley and Mossend of just over 8 hours made rail a viable proposition for time-sensitive traffics that were previously captive to road. One flow

AFTER SPEEDLINK

from Trostre and Ebbw Vale to Westhoughton, anthracite from Onllwyn to Mossend, steel reinforcing bars from Cardiff to Warrington, and steel coil from Port Talbot to Wakefield. Transrail also restarted a regular freight service on the Far North line for the first time in many years, carrying containerised coal to Wick and Thurso and steel to Georgemas Junction for Norfrost. The return working carried Norfrost freezers as well as scrap metal from Thurso.

Transrail's strategy was to add Enterprise services wherever viable traffic volumes were on offer. This included making incursions into areas that were mainly Loadhaul or Mainline Freight territory. Already it hauled calcium carbonate from Quidhampton to Sittingbourne via its Willesden hub, a journey that was entirely on Mainline Freight ground. Transrail identified good potential for wagonload traffic to and from the North East ports, while in the South East it talked of dovetailing with RfD's Connectrail service for train ferry and Channel Tunnel flows.

Cooperation with RfD was already happening on a limited scale, such as the Enterprise service to Aberdeen, which conveyed Connectrail as well as domestic traffic.

●

The takeover of all three former Trainload Freight companies by English Welsh & Scottish Railway (EWS) in 1996, under the leadership of Ed Burkhardt, made it easier for Enterprise to expand into the south and east of the country. The concept of a nationwide less-than-trainload network fitted neatly into EWS's strategy, as the company regarded the trainload market as largely mature, but saw potential in moving lorry-sized loads.

In January 1997 EWS introduced a new train plan for North East England, with a single out-and-back train between Lackenby and Warrington calling at Tees Yard, Healey Mills and Blackburn on the outward run and additionally at Wakefield Cobra on the return. This service made efficiency

No 31203 awaits departure from Queenborough with 6U80, the 1510 Sheerness to Hoo Junction trip, on 19 July 1999. The traffic comprises steel from Sheerness and empty calcium carbonate tanks from Sittingbourne.

At Tilbury Grain Terminal, vans bringing paper from UPM-Kymmene at Irvine for export were backloaded with imported pulp for Iggesund at Workington. No 08531 shunts IZA vans at the terminal on 29 July 1999.

RAIL FREIGHT: WAGONLOAD

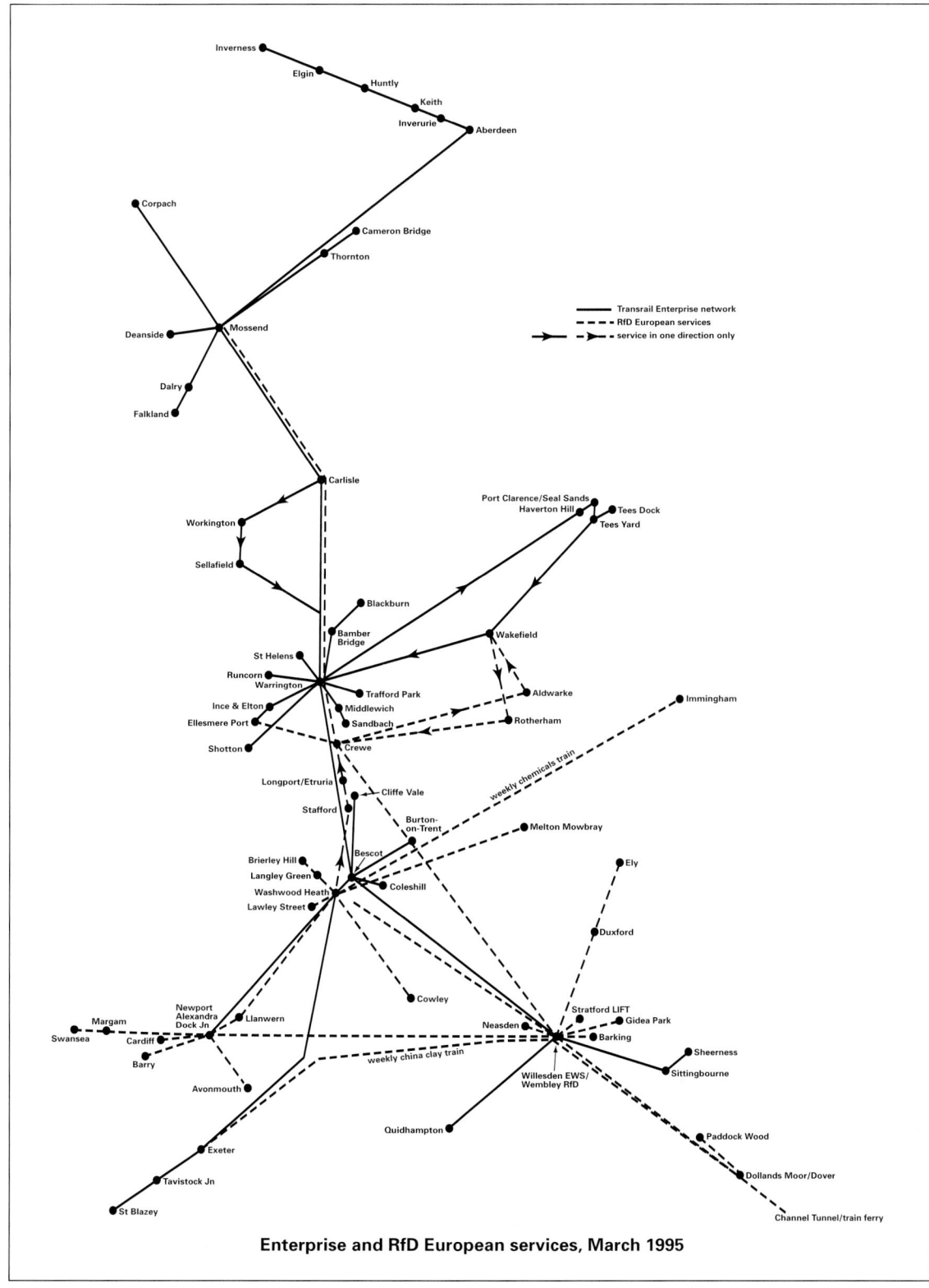

Enterprise and RfD European services, March 1995

AFTER SPEEDLINK

Scheduled Enterprise flows, March 1995

From	To	Traffic	Wagons per day and type
Inverness, Elgin, Huntly and Inverurie	Shotton	Timber	15 OTA
Aberdeen Waterloo	Sittingbourne	Calcium carbonate	1 JCA
Cameron Bridge	Willesden	Carbon dioxide	8 TTA
Oxwellmains	Aberdeen	Cement	12 PCA
Killoch	Keith	Coal	5 HCA
Carlisle	Deanside	Empty, after repair	2 VGA
Workington	Tees Dock	Rail	4 YAA
Seal Sands	Dalry	Caustic soda	2 TTA
Haverton Hill	Coleshill	Carbon dioxide	3 TTA
Trafford Park	Thornton	Starch	1 JBA
Trafford Park	Corpach	Starch	1 PCA
Trafford Park	Sittingbourne	Starch	2 JBA
St Helens	Dalry	Sulphuric acid	1 TIA
Runcorn Folly Lane	Dalry	Salt	2 PGA
Middlewich	Dalry	Salt	2 PGA
Ellesmere Port	Sellafield	Caustic soda	3 TUA
Ince & Elton	Sellafield	Nitric acid	3 TEA
Sandbach	Dalry	Caustic soda	1 TTA
Park Royal	Deanside	Guinness	2 IZA
Cardiff	Warrington Dallam	Coiled steel wire	6 SPA
Burngullow	Aberdeen	China clay	1 ICA
Burngullow	Corpach	China clay	1 TUA
Burngullow	Mossend	China clay	1 TIA
Burngullow	Sittingbourne	China clay	1 TIA
Quidhampton	Mossend	Calcium carbonate	1 ICA
Quidhampton	Corpach	Calcium carbonate	1 ICA
Sheerness	Mossend	Steel reinforcing bar	4 ZAA
Sheerness	Blackburn	Steel reinforcing bar	4 ZAA
Sheerness	Burton-on-Trent	Steel reinforcing bar	4 ZAA

Above In the Burkhardt era EWS found creative solutions for new business opportunities, sometimes bringing long-disused sidings back into use for revenue-earning traffic. At Pontrilas the refurbishment of a single siding provided a convenient offloading point for timber to a local merchant, Pontrilas Timber. The siding was served by a trip working that used a Rail Express Systems Class 47 in marginal time. On 17 July 1997 No 47741 positions five OTAs in the new siding after working the 6C38 trip from Alexandra Dock Junction.

Right Timber from Arrochar and Beattock is unloaded from OTA wagons at the Kronospan factory, Chirk, on 6 August 1999.

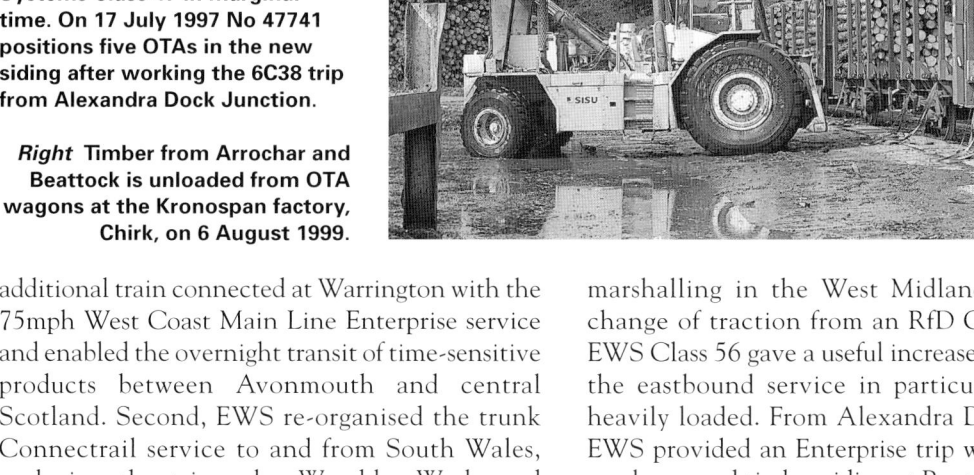

additional train connected at Warrington with the 75mph West Coast Main Line Enterprise service and enabled the overnight transit of time-sensitive products between Avonmouth and central Scotland. Second, EWS re-organised the trunk Connectrail service to and from South Wales, replacing the triangular Wembley-Washwood Heath-Alexandra Dock Junction-Wembley itinerary with a two-way service between Wembley and Alexandra Dock Junction. The change of routeing cut out wasteful mileage and marshalling in the West Midlands, while the change of traction from an RfD Class 47 to an EWS Class 56 gave a useful increase in capacity as the eastbound service in particular was often heavily loaded. From Alexandra Dock Junction EWS provided an Enterprise trip working to the newly opened timber siding at Pontrilas.

In North West England EWS diverted the Sandbach trip working to call at Crewe for Connectrail traffic to the Stevenston distribution depot. The trip to Dee Marsh Junction was

Above Doncaster Belmont yard became the focus for Enterprise trains on the East Coast Main Line and to and from the East Coast ports. On 25 April 2001 No 08587 shunts IWA/IWB vans and TTA tanks at Belmont just after their arrival on the afternoon Enterprise service from Immingham.

Below Heavy loadings justified the diagramming of a Class 60 on the morning Enterprise service to Immingham. No 60012 passes Scunthorpe with 6D65, the 1007 departure from Doncaster Belmont, on 23 July 2003, with a typical mixture of vans, steel carriers, intermodal wagons and oil tanks in tow.

AFTER SPEEDLINK

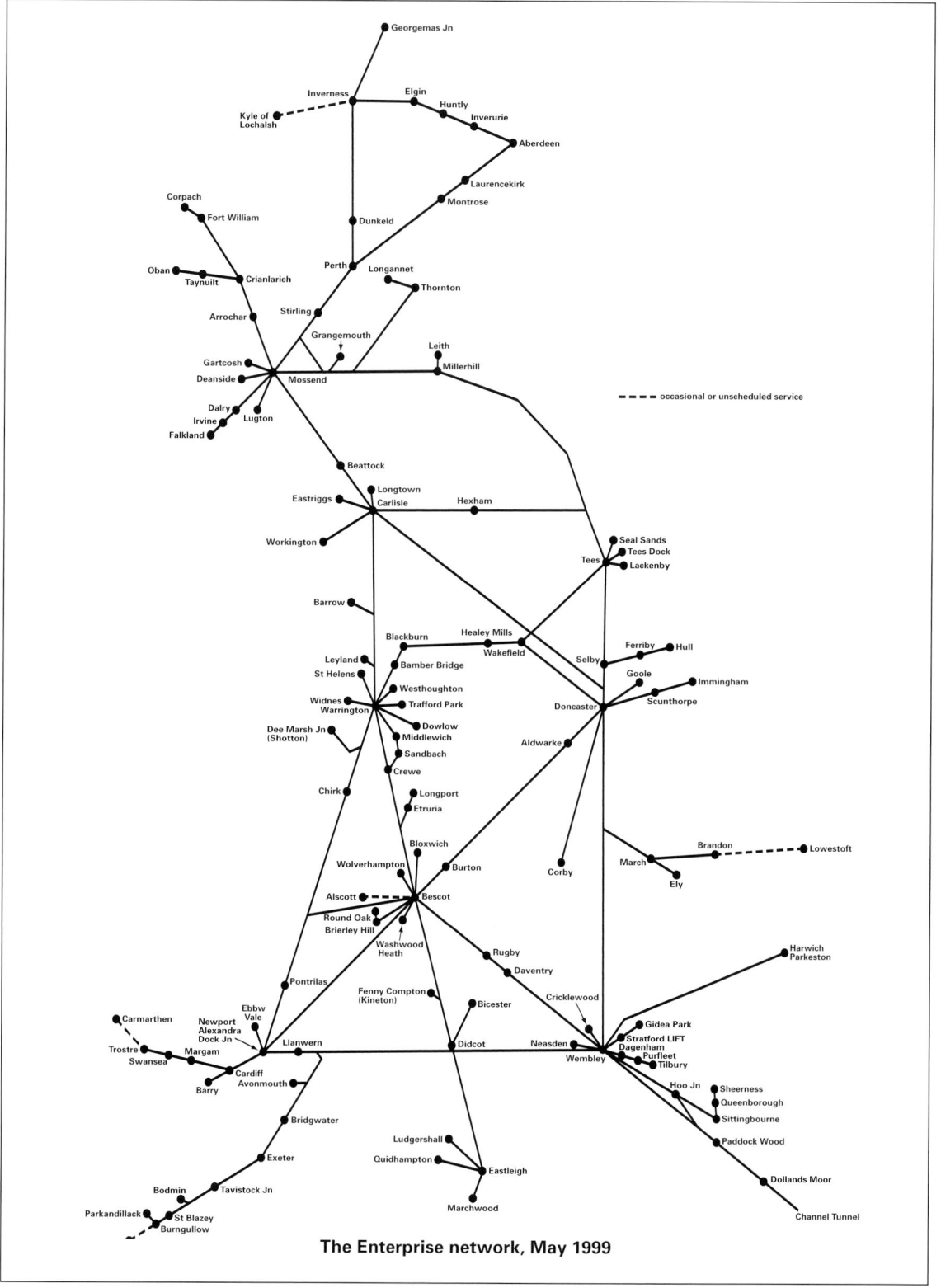

The Enterprise network, May 1999

RAIL FREIGHT: WAGONLOAD

rescheduled as a through train from Mossend to cater for increased volumes of timber to Shotton Paper. The Kronospan factory at Chirk regained a rail service, both for inward timber and for outward trial movements of finished product.

EWS introduced its first East Coast Main Line Enterprise service in June 1997, linking Tees, Millerhill, Thornton, Montrose and Aberdeen. The initial flows on this train were lime from Thrislington to Montrose and cement from Oxwellmains to Aberdeen. In August the train was extended southwards to run to and from Wakefield, mainly to cater for a new flow of Superdrug products from Wakefield to the rail-served TDG Harris warehouse at Mossend. The service also carried containers from Tees Dock to Mossend for P&O and North Sea Ferries.

Timber traffic from Scotland and the border counties continued to grow. Among the new loading points established in 1997 were Laurencekirk, Dunkeld, Beattock, Carlisle Upperby and Hexham. The siding at Hexham was also used as a receiving point for timber to the nearby Egger factory. In the North of Scotland, the increase in timber and other wagonload traffic led to the introduction of a second daily Enterprise train between Aberdeen and Elgin and a second daily train between Mossend and Fort William. EWS also ran special trains for spot loads of timber from Kyle of Lochalsh and Dunrobin.

The years 1998 and 1999 saw further growth for Enterprise. In May 1998 Doncaster Belmont yard was refettled to supersede Healey Mills as the major hub for Yorkshire and the East Coast ports. Its location on the East Coast Main Line gave it a strategic advantage compared with Healey Mills. It was served by trunk trains to Harwich, Wembley, Bescot, Warrington, Tees and Aberdeen, with feeder services to Selby, Hull, Immingham, Wakefield, Aldwarke and Ely. From 1999 Doncaster was served by a new trunk service linking Corby with Mossend via the Settle & Carlisle line and by a diverted metals service between Lackenby and Margam.

Those years brought numerous new wagonload flows to fuel the expansion of the network, and for a time Enterprise looked to be heading towards a reincarnation of Speedlink. Grain traffic returned, with a 12-week contract from Andover to Roseisle using six IRB wagons that had been imported from France. Animal feeds were carried from Ely to Scotland and, on a trial basis, from New Holland to Selby. EWS even carried a few vanloads of seed potatoes on routes such as Inverness to Thornaby, Inverness to Selby, Inverness to Ely, Elgin to Rugby, and Aberdeen to St Blazey – the first time that this traffic had moved by rail since the 1980s.

In the forest products sector, EWS gained a regular flow of pulp from Sheerness to Barrow-in-

Class 92 electric locomotives were finally authorised to work freight trains between Crewe and Mossend in the summer of 1998. No 92024 pulls out of Mossend yard on 14 July 1998 with 6M27, the 1515 service to Bescot, conveying VGA vans loaded with Spillers petfood for Wisbech. The Spillers traffic had previously operated as a full trainload but now used Enterprise as far as Warrington because of reduced volumes.

AFTER SPEEDLINK

Furness for Kimberly Clark and short-term pulp movements from Aberdeen, Montrose, Dundee and Grangemouth to Corpach for Arjo Wiggins. Some of the wagons that carried pulp from Tilbury to Workington for Iggesund were backloaded with finished product for export. The well-established trainload flow of imported newsprint from Immingham to Barking for Stora Enso celebrated its millionth tonne in 1997, and Stora Enso also used Enterprise to carry paper from Immingham to Glasgow Deanside. Import flows via the Channel Tunnel included paper reels from Germany and Austria to various terminals including Stratford and Ely, and chipboard from Austria to Selby, from where it was delivered by road to Hygena at Howden and Egger at Hexham.

Home-produced paper was forwarded from Aberdeen for International Paper to France via the Channel Tunnel and in containers to Belgium via Purfleet. There was also domestic container traffic from Aberdeen to Ely and Daventry. Arjo Wiggins at Corpach produced a regular flow to Cardiff and occasional traffic to Avonmouth and Purfleet. Caledonian Paper at Irvine dispatched

Right Imported pulp for Kimberly Clark at Barrow-in-Furness is loaded into IWA/IWB vans at Sheerness on 19 July 1999. At that time EWS operated a daily trunk Enterprise service from Hoo Junction to Barrow-in-Furness, mainly for the pulp traffic.

Below Although well outside the original Transrail Enterprise network, Immingham became one of the busiest locations in the country for EWS Enterprise traffic. No 08886 shunts vans loaded with Stora Enso paper at Immingham reception sidings on 7 August 2002.

RAIL FREIGHT: WAGONLOAD

paper to Antwerp via the Channel Tunnel and to Purfleet for local distribution. EWS also won a substantial two-way flow between Irvine and Shotton, with magazine paper moving from Irvine to Shotton for the English and Welsh market and newsprint moving from Shotton to Irvine for the Scottish market.

Raw timber continued to thrive, too. EWS reached an estimated market share of 80%-90% of long-distance flows from loading points north of the Central Belt, reducing to 40% from the Scottish Borders. Alongside the established traffic to Shotton, Chirk and Pontrilas, EWS moved logs to Boat of Garten, Carlisle, Hereford and Cardiff for BSW, to Elgin for James Jones, and to Nairn for Gordons. The list of loading points continued to grow, with the following all in use at some point in 1998/99:

Thurso • Kyle of Lochalsh • Inverness • Elgin • Huntly • Inverurie • Laurencekirk • Dunkeld • Stirling • Fort William • Oban • Taynuilt • Crianlarich • Arrochar • Deanside • Irvine • Beattock • Carlisle Upperby • Hexham • Tees Yard • Brandon • Eastleigh • Exeter Riverside

At its peak the timber-carrying business required the use not only of EWS's 250 OTA stanchioned timber wagons but also of OBA open wagons and bogie IGA and IOB flat wagons hired from GE Rail Services.

The Ministry of Defence increased its use of rail, especially after the formation of the Defence Logistics Organisation, which combined the logistics wings of the three armed forces. The MoD signed a new five-year contract with EWS in 1999 to cover a daily wagonload service on the core network and special trainload movements as required. The MoD's Longtown depot benefited from a new £5.5 million road-rail transfer facility. Several abandoned lines and terminals were brought back into use, with the Redmire branch

A temporary freight renaissance on the Highland main line: Rail Express Systems-liveried locomotive No 47501 enters Mossend up reception sidings with 6D46, the 1330 departure from Inverness, on 15 July 1998. The load comprises OTAs with timber to Shotton, IWB vans with barrels of aviation fuel to Immingham, PFAs with empty coal containers to Gascoigne Wood, and one VGA van with mineral water to Dagenham. Five years later, none of these flows would remain on rail.

Some former RfD trains retained Class 47 haulage under EWS management. No 47311 passes Northam steel terminal on the approach to Southampton with 6B45, the 0744 Eastleigh to Marchwood trip, on 20 July 1998. The train is conveying mainly VGA vans with military stores.

handling military vehicles for Catterick garrison and the Mid-Norfolk Railway line to East Dereham used for traffic to the nearby Robertson barracks. The rail connection to Ashchurch was restored and special trains reached 'off the beaten track' locations including Pembroke Dock, Caerwent, Wool and Shoeburyness.

While Channel Tunnel intermodal traffic declined, the tonnage of international freight handled in conventional wagons held up well. Operations on the British side of the Channel were helped by the full integration of all Enterprise and Connectrail services. In December 1998 EWS introduced a direct wagonload service between Britain and Köln Gremberg yard, cutting out the need for time-consuming marshalling in France and giving greatly improved journey times to and from Germany. The Europe-bound train was heavily loaded with steel from Port Talbot, Llanwern and Rotherham, while the return service carried flows such as chemicals from Ludwigshafen to Immingham, coiled steel rod from Duisburg to Longport, chipboard from Brilon to Selby, and aluminium from Singen to Wolverhampton.

Most promisingly of all, EWS seemed to be claiming a meaningful toehold in the highly prized fast-moving consumer goods market, especially the food and drink sector. With 300 million tonnes of food and drink consumed in Britain each year, even a small increase in the railway's market share would be significant. EWS used conventional vans to convey palletised goods for Superdrug from Wakefield to Mossend and from Mossend to Hoo Junction, for Sainsbury between Mossend and Dagenham, and for Safeway to and from Hoo Junction, Daventry, Wakefield and Mossend. Intermodal transport offered further opportunities, including the ground-breaking service carrying temperature-controlled swapbodies for Safeway from Mossend to Inverness, later extended to Georgemas Junction.

●

It was all too good to last! In July 1999 the charismatic Ed Burkhardt was ejected from the EWS board and the company's aspiration to treble rail freight in ten years was quickly forgotten. In particular, doubts were expressed – not for the first time – about the viability of wagonload in a small country such as Britain. On the ground, the number of new wagonload flows diminished almost to zero, and there were a worrying number of losses, some brought about by the customer for whom road transport could offer a cheaper and/or more reliable service and others brought about by EWS as it sought to eliminate uneconomic trip workings. Some flows were doubtless casualties of the delays that followed the Hatfield derailment in October 2000. Any new traffic that might previously have gone by Enterprise tended to be conveyed instead by block trains and customer-specific feeder services, with minimal shunting or marshalling en route.

During 2001 EWS maintained its core Enterprise network, despite fears among customers that its demise was imminent. However, further traffic losses led to consistently poor loadings on some trunk services, while a number of local trip

RAIL FREIGHT: WAGONLOAD

EWS provided a small fleet of refurbished CSA tank wagons to transport lime from Dowlow to the re-opened Fifoots Point power station. Pilot locomotive No L106 shunts four CSAs at Fifoots Point on 26 October 2000.

The Potter Group established a major railhead at Knowsley at a time when other rail terminal operators were struggling to stay in business. The main traffic was imported paper from Immingham for Stora Enso. Resident pilot locomotive No 08202 shunts empty IWB vans at Knowsley on 21 August 2001.

Sentinel 0-6-0 locomotive with maker's number 10220 waits in the unloading shed at the Potter Group railhead at Selby on 13 June 2002. At that time the Selby terminal received a daily trainload of paper from Felixstowe, a daily trainload of paper from Immingham, a three-times-weekly GB Railfreight intermodal service from Felixstowe, a twice-weekly stone train from Peak Forest and a daily Enterprise service from Doncaster.

AFTER SPEEDLINK

workings were withdrawn completely, especially those serving the extremities of the network such as Cornwall and parts of the Scottish Highlands. Among the many lost flows were Cerestar starch from Trafford Park, pulp to Barrow-in-Furness, Workington and Corpach, finished products from Workington and Corpach, Fitzgerald lighting products from Bodmin, bottled mineral water from Inverness, Spillers petfood between Deanside and Wisbech, and all raw timber traffic except from the West Highland line and Carlisle to Chirk and occasional trainloads from the lineside loading point at Kinbrace to Inverness.

But not all the news was bad. One Enterprise customer that bucked the trend was Stora Enso, which now used a combination of trainload and Enterprise services to move imported paper from Immingham, Felixstowe and Zeebrugge to distribution terminals at Barking, Selby, Knowsley, Avonmouth and Deanside. Tying in with the increased paper traffic was the Potter Group's new Knowsley railhead, opened in 2001 to complement its existing Ely and Selby terminals. EWS provided a daily service to Knowsley, which could convey general wagonload traffic from mainland Europe as well as the core flow of paper from Immingham.

Other bright spots in 2002 were the re-opening of the Runcorn Folly Lane branch for caustic soda traffic from Ineos Chlor, part funded by a £4 million Freight Facilities Grant, and the upgrading of the Thurso branch for wagonloads of building materials to Thurso Building Supplies, supported by a £289,000 grant. Unfortunately the Thurso traffic was to cease in 2004 following the loss of the Safeway business that travelled on the same train.

Just when it seemed that Enterprise was stabilising, the near total stoppage of Channel Tunnel freight in November 2001 caused by waves of asylum-seekers seeking entry to the UK dealt a cruel blow to EWS's European arm, wiping out numerous flows overnight while trains were barred from using the Tunnel and causing long-term damage to the business. Among the railheads that closed in the wake of the crisis were the Creative Logistics depot at Salford, opened as recently as 2000, the DCA Link terminal at Cardiff Canton, and the EWS terminal at Longport. A number of small flows were either slow to return to rail or did not return at all.

Nevertheless, the Volkswagen Audi Group pressed ahead with its plans to establish a rail-served depot for imported vehicle parts at Birch

Below left Creative Logistics brought rail traffic back to the former Otis distribution terminal at Ordsall Lane, Salford. The company's smartly painted pilot locomotive No 01552 shunts IWA vans loaded with tissues from Crailsheim on 22 May 2001. Unfortunately the Creative Logistics operation was soon to become a casualty of the asylum-seekers crisis.

Below right Wagon labels remained in use for European traffic long after they were discontinued on most domestic flows. The data on this label pictured at Ordsall Lane on 22 May 2001 include the wagon number (3380 269 3005-1, top right), the number of axles on the wagon (4), the name of consignee (P&G = Procter & Gamble, Skelmersdale, top left), the destination station (Manchester Ordsall), the destination country code and location code (70-291302), and details of the routeing through Germany, Belgium and France (8050-1, 8816, 8765).

RAIL FREIGHT: WAGONLOAD

Nos 92012 and 92010 await departure from Frethun with vans containing mineral water for Neasden on 31 May 2001. Once in Britain, the train will travel forward as 6B50, the 2015 from Dollands Moor to Wembley.

Coppice, and the re-opened 3-mile branch from Kingsbury carried its first revenue-earning train in the summer of 2002. Corus meanwhile used EWS to carry trainloads of steel from Lackenby and Scunthorpe to Ébange via the Tunnel, with a three-year contract taking effect from late 2003.

In 2004/05 the Enterprise network was showing encouraging signs of recovery, with most trunk trains carrying traffic that was regular enough to justify the provision of resources but not sufficient to fill a trainload. However, some feeder services ran with very light loads, such as Mossend to Aberdeen, which often carried only a handful of wagons with steel pipes for Laurencekirk, and the Eastleigh to Wembley service, which often consisted of a few tank wagons with gas oil for railway fuelling points.

EWS continued to shift business between trainload and Enterprise operation where it made sense to do so. In September 2004 it replaced the St Blazey to Cliffe Vale clay train and occasional block loads of scrap metal from Plymouth to Cardiff with a single train from Tavistock Junction to Cardiff Tidal conveying clay, scrap metal and any other available freight; however, the loaded clay and scrap metal trains later reverted to separate operation with only the southbound empties running as a combined service via Cardiff.

The flow of imported steel coil from Victa Railfreight at Hoo Junction to Wolverhampton transferred from block train to Enterprise in 2003, giving the customer a more frequent service. The export steel from Lackenby and Scunthorpe to Mostyn was combined with the paper from Immingham to Knowsley for part of its journey in order to cut out wasteful duplication. The weekly trainload of china clay from Cornwall to Sezzadio became an Enterprise movement in 2005, with the

AFTER SPEEDLINK

Vintage traction on a newly re-opened freight-only branch: No 37042 departs from Birch Coppice exchange sidings with 6G42, the 1130 Enterprise trip working to Bescot, on 23 October 2002.

loaded wagons routed via Eastleigh and Wembley and the return empties routed via Wembley and Cardiff. Fuel oil from Grangemouth to Sinfin became an Enterprise movement as far as Doncaster, with a weekly feeder service from Doncaster to Sinfin. EWS continued to move occasional consignments of contaminated drill cuttings from Aberdeen and Hamworthy to Lowestoft, using Enterprise services to Wembley and special trains as required from Wembley to Lowestoft.

Stora Enso changed its distribution arrangements in 2005, withdrawing from Felixstowe and setting up a new import terminal at Tilbury. Much of the former Felixstowe traffic now travelled by rail from Tilbury instead, but the Channel Tunnel flow from Zeebrugge to Barking ceased. Elsewhere in the paper industry, UPM-Kymmene continued to dispatch paper by rail from Irvine to Daventry but ended the two-way traffic between Irvine and Shotton.

Some Enterprise traffic was lost not through any fault of EWS but because of changes in the industries that it served – illustrating the point that the railway has to continue finding new business just to stand still in terms of overall tonnage. The long-established flow of white goods to Paddock Wood ended abruptly in 2005 following a major warehouse fire, while the last remaining freight flow to Corpach – calcium carbonate from Quidhampton – ceased when the Arjo Wiggins plant closed in September 2005. On the positive side, EWS established a new railhead in conjunction with Victa Railfreight at Ridham Dock to receive building materials from Germany, and rail traffic from the Anglesey Aluminium plant at Holyhead resumed with a weekly consignment of billet to Austria.

●

What future for wagonload freight? The key to success is the containment of costs, by reducing intermediate marshalling to an absolute minimum

RAIL FREIGHT: WAGONLOAD

After the end of timber traffic to Shotton, EWS continued to run a daily Enterprise train between Warrington and Dee Marsh Junction for the two-way flow of paper between Irvine and Shotton. No 66062 passes Chester on 3 July 2001 with four IZA twin vans forming 6F62, the 1230 Dee Marsh Junction to Warrington Arpley.

Because of the restrictions on dangerous goods using the Channel Tunnel, very little chemical traffic between Britain and mainland Europe remained on rail after the withdrawal of the train ferry. However, in early 2005 the AHC terminal at Widnes picked up a new international flow in VTG-owned ICB tank wagons. No 66139 heads east on the low-level line at Warrington Arpley on 5 April with three ICB tanks and one FCA twin set loaded with tanktainers, forming 6F01, the 0820 Arpley to Ditton.

Above The loss of the Royal Mail contract left EWS with plenty of spare capacity in its Class 67 fleet. Some Class 67s were redeployed on lightly loaded freight workings, including Enterprise trips from Bescot, Warrington, Doncaster and Mossend. No 67003 takes the west-facing curve at Northwich South Junction on 8 April 2005 with 6F17, the 1110 Sandbach to Warrington Arpley trip, conveying three TEA tanks with hydrochloric acid for Dalry.

Below No 92034 passes Stableford with 6S75, the 1807 Bescot to Mossend trunk Enterprise service, on 27 June 2005. The consist includes one IZA van with imported chipboard for Deanside, 14 OBA and one SPA wagons returning from Lowestoft to Aberdeen after carrying contaminated drill cuttings, two empty IWB vans from Avonmouth to Grangemouth, and one empty IZA van from Daventry to Irvine.

RAIL FREIGHT: WAGONLOAD

and ensuring adequate loadings on all trunk trains and trip workings. A study publicised by the Rail Freight Group in 2002 suggested that the best hope for a wagonload renaissance lay in persuading different freight operators to work together more closely, pooling their traction and train crew resources on specified routes and conveying each others' traffic in order to ensure viable loadings. However, the study recognised the limitations of such a scheme: it may be difficult in practice to reconcile the different needs of different traffic flows in terms of train speed, departure or arrival time and overall duration of journey. And any combined operations would require additional shunting, adding to the overall costs.

In practice, competing freight operators have shown little interest in pooling resources. In 2005 the rail freight flows to Aberdeen were divided between no fewer than four operators: Freightliner Heavy Haul for cement, DRS for containers, GB Railfreight for petroleum products, and EWS for the residual wagonload business. The first three companies all hauled viable trainloads and had nothing to gain from sharing. A similar situation existed on the North Wales coast, where Freightliner carried ballast, DRS nuclear flasks and EWS occasional loads of aluminium and stone. Here the three companies served different terminals from each other, often on different days of the week, and it would be costly and time-consuming for them to combine haulage.

Nevertheless, EWS Chief Executive Keith Heller spoke in 2005 of his desire for wagonload growth, using words that seemed to echo those uttered by Ed Burkhardt eight years earlier. In October 2005 the Freight Transport Association and Rail Freight Group published a document entitled 'Forecasts of future demand for rail freight', which confirmed the potential for substantial growth in intermodal and wagonload traffic: Channel Tunnel volumes could expect to rise from 2.0 to 7.2 million tonnes between 2003 and 2014 and domestic non-bulk traffic from 0.9 to 4.7 million tonnes in the same period.

Perhaps the closest thing to a wagonload service operated by a freight company other than EWS is the twice-weekly chemicals train to Sellafield run by Direct Rail Services. In 2005 this train was sometimes routed via both Runcorn and Sandbach to collect tankloads of caustic soda and nitric acid respectively. Even when it served only one location it looked more like a wagonload trip than a trainload service. Nos 37069 and 37259 approach the Ineos Chlor terminal at Runcorn Folly Lane with 6P25, the 0559 departure from Sellafield, on 5 April 2005.

Index

Aberdeen 78
Acton yard 11
Air-braked wagons 11, 17, 29, 32, 46, 47, 48; 'fitted head' 11, 47
Alexandra Dock Junction yard 111
Aluminium traffic 18, 27, 54
Auchmuty branch 77
Avonmouth 65

Beeching Report, 1963 7, 16, 26, 29, 33, 89
Bescot yard 94, 95, 112
Bicester 100, 101, 102; see also Military traffic
Birch Coppice exchange sidings 123
Blackburn 74
Bletchley flyover 7
Boston Docks 52
Bow yard 76
Brake-vans 31, 32, 37, 48, 77
Bridgwater 19
Burkhardt, Ed 109, 119, 126
Burton-on-Trent 106
Butterley Brick 55, 57

Cambrian Coast line 18, 22
Cambridge Coalfields terminal 38ff
Car traffic 103, 121
Cargowaggon vans 48
Carlisle Kingmoor yard 7, 62, 64
Cement traffic 9, 103
Cerestar 73, 104, 121
Channel Tunnel 83, 96, 119, 121, 122, 124, 126
Chemical traffic 1, 23, 24, 38, 44, 76, 79, 83ff, 94, 95, 96, 97, 98, 100, 124, 125
China clay traffic 23, 54, 64, 73, 77, 86, 94, 99, 100, 122
Ciba-Geigy 24, 25, 44, 52, 83ff, 94, 97
Cider traffic 52, 100, 103, 106
Coal traffic 11, 26, 30, 38, 50, 64, 105
'Conflat' wagons 9, 15

Connectrail 109ff
Containers 9, 29; see also Freightliner
'Contract' trains 96ff
Creative Logistics, Salford 121
Crewe 95, 96
Croes Newydd yard 19

Departmental traffic/Civilink 30, 94, 99
Derwent Valley Light Railway 28
Doncaster Belmont yard 114, 116
Donnington exchange sidings 75
Dover 80, 81
Dumfries 27
Dunkerque 82, 83
Duxford see Ciba-Geigy

English Welsh & Scottish Railway 109ff, 126
Enterprise 104ff, 110ff, 125; flows, 1995 107, 108; network, 1999 115
European traffic 89ff, 96, 108, 112; see also Train ferries
Explosives traffic 22, 54, 57

Fakenham branch 16, 18, 51
Falkland Junction yard, Ayr 61, 66
Far North line 26, 109
Ferry vans 23, 38, 44, 46, 48, 49, 54, 57, 67, 78, 92, 94, 95, 96; see also Train ferries
Fish traffic 26
Food and drink traffic 44, 52, 53, 103, 119, 122
Forfar branch 27
Freightliner 29, 67, 73, 95, 102
Fruit traffic 23
Furzebrook 77

Gidea Park terminal 112
Gloucester yard 66
Goods yards, closure of 16, 25
Grain traffic 30, 50, 85, 103, 109, 116

Grangemouth 78
Guinness 47, 52

Healey Mills yard 47, 105, 116
Hereford 75
Hoo Junction yard 63
Hump shunting 7, 31, 32, 36, 38, 47, 62

Immingham 110, 117
'Insulfish' vans 15, 26
Interfrigo vans 51
Invergordon 4, 27

LCP distribution terminal 55
Lime traffic 21
Loadhaul 104, 109
Locomotives: Clayton Type 1 15; Class 08 19, 38, 39; Class 09 80, 81, 82; Class 15 9; Class 20 16; Class 67 125
Longport freight terminal 95

Mainline Freight 104, 109
Marshalling instructions, examples of 12-14
Marshalling yards 47, 62
Menstrie branch 51
Metal Box 47, 48, 49
Military traffic 40, 43, 50, 64, 75, 100, 101, 102, 118-119
Mixed goods/passenger trains 26
Modernisation Plan, 1955 7, 31
Mossend yard 116, 118

New England yard, Peterborough 17

Oil traffic 26, 67, 77, 104

Paper traffic 73, 78, 117, 118, 120, 121, 123, 124
Parker, Sir Peter 46, 49
Petfood traffic 51, 54, 94, 116

RAIL FREIGHT: WAGONLOAD

'Pick-up' goods trains 16, 18, 22
'Polybulk' wagons 50, 51, 52, 85, 86, 88
Pontrilas 113
Potato traffic 27, 44, 45, 50, 116
Potter Group 45, 52, 94, 120, 121
'Presflo' wagons 9
Private sidings 52, 54, 55, 63
Privately owned wagons 46, 50
'Public delivery sidings' 24, 44
Public freight terminals 16, 27, 63
Pulp traffic 56, 116-117

Queenborough 109

Rail Freight Group 104, 126
Railfreight sectors 64, 65
Railfreight Distribution 38, 64, 65, 67, 73, 88, 89, 92, 93, 95, 96, 100, 103, 108, 111
Road connections 24
Rowntrees 52, 53, 57
Russell, J. G. 52, 54

St Blazey yard 54
Scrap metal traffic 30, 31, 65, 106, 122

'Sectorisation' of freight 64
Settle & Carlisle line 7, 10, 49
Severn Tunnel Junction yard 47, 62, 64
Sheerness 112, 117
Sheffield Freight Terminal 24
Sittingbourne 100, 112
Speedlink 11, 29, 30, 37, 38, 46ff, 86, 87; end of 38, 78, 79, 87, 89ff; flows 1990-91 69-73; Manchester area trips 61-62; network 57-61, 68; 'Network 90' 67, 73, 78; replacement services, 1991 90-91, 104ff; speed of 50; Speedlink Distribution 52; Speedlink Review 1990 73
Steel traffic 40, 65, 105, 122
Stranraer 66
Swanbourne, proposed yard 7

Tees Yard 31ff; trips from, 1979 34-35
Temple Mills yard 11, 61, 66, 76, 88, 89
Tiger Rail/Tiger Freightways 96ff
Tilbury 109
Timber traffic 56, 57, 73, 97, 100, 103, 106, 113, 116, 118

TOPS scheme 46
Trafford Park Estates 73
Train ferries 8, 67, 74, 80ff; 'Night Ferry' 80; *Nord Pas-de-Calais* 67, 80, 82, 83
Trainload Construction 103-104
Trainload Freight 89, 94, 104, 109
Trainload Metals 94, 105
Trainload Petroleum 88, 104
Transrail 104, 105, 106, 109
'Trip' workings 11, 15, 16, 17, 21, 28, 29, 33, 34-35, 38, 56, 65, 93; Manchester area examples 20-22
12-ton vans, standard 17, 45

Wagonload traffic, decline of 7, 16, 24, 30, 38, 46, 50, 83; future for 123ff
Warrington yards 74, 79, 124
Wembley European Freight Operation Centre 112
West Highland line 18, 26, 56
Whisky traffic 3, 27, 67
Whitehaven 23
Whitemoor yard 47
Whittlesford *see* Ciba-Geigy